Capital Punishment:
The Inevitability
of Caprice and Mistake

CHARLES L. BLACK Jr.

Capital Punishment:
The Inevitability
of Caprice and Mistake

Second Edition
Augmented

W · W · NORTON & COMPANY
NEW YORK   LONDON

Copyright © 1981, 1974 by W. W. Norton & Company, Inc.
Copyright © 1977, 1978 by Charles L. Black, Jr.

Printed in the United States of America.

First Edition

Library of Congress Cataloging in Publication Data

Black, Charles Lund, 1915–
    Capital punishment.

    1. Capital punishment.   I. Title.
HV8698.B47 1981   364.6'6   81–2824
ISBN 0-393-01333-2
ISBN 0-393-95289-4 {pbk.}   AACR2

W. W. Norton & Company, Inc., 500 Fifth Avenue, New York, N.Y. 10110
W. W. Norton & Company Ltd., 10 Coptic Street, London, WC1A 1PU

5 6 7 8 9 0

To my brother, Thomas Bowman Black

Contents

Preface to the Second Edition   9

Preface to the First Edition   13

PART I: THE INEVITABILITY OF
            CAPRICE AND MISTAKE IN
            ADMINISTERING THE DEATH
            PENALTY

1.   Introduction   17

2.   Mistake and Arbitrariness—
     An Overview   22

3.   Other Arguments about Capital
     Punishment   31

4.   The Problem of Other Forms of
     Punishment   38

5.   The Decisions on Charging and On
     Plea-Bargaining   46

6.   The Trial and Verdict   54

7.   The Sentence-Choice   65

8.   After Sentencing (Appeal, Post-
      Conviction Remedies, Clemency)   79
9.   Mistake or Uncertainty of Law   85
10.   The Warping Effects of Race and
      Poverty   94
11.   A Summary—Law New
      and Old   103

PART II: THE NEWER PHASE
           1. Due Process for Death: Jurek v.
           Texas and Companion Cases
           (1976)   111
           2. The Death Penalty Now (1977)   135
           3. Reflections on Opposing the
           Penalty of Death (1978)   157

Preface to the Second Edition

THIS NEW EDITION is substantially augmented, rather than revised. Let me clarify and explain this.

Part I of the present edition is simply the text of the first edition. The book has been often cited and quoted; I have thought, therefore, that the confusion that might result from variant texts ought to be avoided, unless new events or insights made change inevitable. Far from this, I find nothing at all in the earlier text from which I would wish to recede. Things stand now as they stood then, with regard to the nature of the standards and processes by which we choose people for death. We have chosen a lot more people for death than had been chosen when the first edition was published; in order to update the book on this and other such peripheral matters, I have added a very few new footnotes. Part I is therefore to be seen as stating the position as it was just *before* the Supreme Court rehabilitated the death penalty, in July, 1976—a position in no way changed, as far as the merits of the matter are concerned.

Part II presents three articles of mine, published in periodicals since the first edition appeared, but nowhere collected. They express my thoughts on this subject *since*

the Supreme Court decisions of July 2, 1976, which vali-
dated several of the death-penalty statutes discussed in
Chapter 7 of the first edition (and therefore of Part I of the
present edition, at p. 65). I have thought that the articles
that form Part II might be of interest to those looking for
more detailed development of certain of the earlier
themes, against the background of the grim imminence
of actual resumption of executions on a large scale.

The division of this edition into two "Parts" is therefore at the crucially important event of July 2, 1976.

The articles forming Part II were delivered as
lectures—*Due Process for Death* as the 1976 Pope John
XXIII Lecture at the Law School of the Catholic University of America, *The Death Penalty Now* as the 1977
George Abel Dreyfous Lecture at the Tulane University
Law School, and *Reflections on Opposing the Penalty of
Death*, at a 1978 lecture at St. Mary's University School
of Law in San Antonio. These lectures were published,
as delivered, in the respective law reviews or journals of
these institutions, and thanks are due to all of them for
permitting, in one way or another, this republication. I
am, indeed, grateful to these three journals for much
help along the way toward first publication, as well as for
permission to reprint.

Due Process for Death, infra, p. 111, is a critique of
the Supreme Court's July, 1976 reasons, as these were
brought forward by the Court to sustain the new death-
penalty statutes.

The Death Penalty Now, infra p. 135, deepens my
critique of the plea-bargaining process in death-cases,
points out some of the truly zany material in the Ohio
death-penalty law, and deals with the utterly erroneous
notion that "the most malignant and abandoned of deliberate killers" are the ones going to death row.

In *Reflections on Opposing the Penalty of Death*, *infra* p. 157, I believe I have deepened the processual approach of the earlier edition—a deepening that came out of years of my taking part in controversy on this subject.

These articles, like the first edition of this book, were events definitely placed in an ongoing controversy of highest seriousness—a controversy not yet ended. I have not wanted to alter them to a timelessness which would be lifelessness, but have left them as they are, each speaking as of its own year, to issues which were before, were then, and are now amongst the most agonizing we will ever face.

I turn with pleasure and fear to the acknowledgment of new debts contracted—pleasure on obvious grounds, and fear that I shall not immediately call to mind some of the help I have received in the six years since the first edition appeared.

Again, "thanks are due and gladly given" to George Brockway of Norton, and to Barbara Aronstein Black, with whom I talked over all the matter in this edition, but whose help was particularly crucial in regard to *Reflections on Opposing the Penalty of Death* in Part II.

New debts are to Elizabeth M. Doyle, who has, as always, most skillfully managed the manuscript; to Professor William Fox and many others at the Catholic University of America's Law School; to Professor Joel Friedman and his colleagues at Tulane; to my brother Professor Thomas B. Black of St. Mary's University Law School (to whom the book is dedicated), and to his colleagues there; to William and Penelope Twining, who were, most luckily for me, around just when I needed them to discuss some passages in *Due Process for Death*; to Henry Schwarzschild and Deborah Leavy; to Hugo

Adam Bedau; to Richard Lempert; to Glenn L. Pierce and William J. Bowers; to Arthur John Keeffe; to Arthur Charpentier; to Milton Heumann; to Seth Waxman.

Of those inadvertently omitted, I ask pardon; six years of travel and talk over and about this subject have left me feeling that I owe more thoughts to more people than I can possibly call to mind in the finite time allowed for compiling a preface. This is always true, as to all one's writings, but more so as to this one than I have ever felt it to be before.

C.L.B., Jr.

Preface to the
First Edition

MY THANKS are due and gladly given to George Brockway, Calvin Towle, and the staff of W. W. Norton & Company; to Eileen M. Quinn and Carolyn B. Vitale, for help that transcended the secretarial; to Robert S. Davis, Yale Law School 1974, who put thought as well as research work into the product; to Dean William P. Cunningham, the University of Maryland Law School, and the Maryland Law Review, for the stimulus given me, in their invitation to deliver the Morris Ames Soper Lecture in 1972, to begin structuring my thought about this subject; to Professor Aaron Schreiber, who led me back to a half-remembered Talmudic reference; to my son Gavin B. Black, who read and helpfully commented on the manuscript; and to Barbara A. Black, with whom I have talked much on these matters. I ought also to say, though I cannot trace the exact line of indebtedness, that my thoughts on discretion and mistake owe much to the work, and to the conversation in years past, of Professor Ronald Dworkin. I also owe a general indebtedness to Professor Guido Calabresi, to Professor Jay Katz, M.D., and to Edward W. Allen, M.D., with all of whom I have so thoroughly traveled over the subject of the penalty of death. My particular debt to Dean Abraham Goldstein is specifically acknowledged in Chapter 6; my whole debt to him is more general. None of these of course is responsible for anything, except as one is necessarily responsible for the ideas one stimulates in the minds of one's friends.

C. L. B., Jr.

Part I: The Inevitability of Caprice and Mistake in Administering the Death Penalty

Chapter 1

Introduction

ALTHOUGH quite different and (to the public taste) more sensationally absorbing events have eclipsed the fact, this country is now in the midst of a great moral crisis, a crisis concerning the punishment of death. Though I oppose the death penalty on many grounds, this book deals with just two aspects of the death-penalty problem—the possibility of *mistake* in the infliction of this penalty and the presence of standardless *arbitrariness* in its infliction. I shall try to show that these two facets of the problem are in some sense the same or, at least, that they are so indissolubly connected as often to be indistinguishable. Though I hope some enlightenment may be a by-product, my aim is to persuade you that these two problems—mistake and arbitrariness in death-penalty cases—are not fringe-problems, susceptible to being mopped up by minor refinements in concept and technique, but are at the very heart of the matter and are insoluble by any methods now known or now foreseeable. If we resume use of the death penalty, we will be killing some people by mistake and some without application of comprehensible standards, and we will go on doing these things until we give up the death penalty.

Let me first sketch the immediate background, hardly old enough to be called history. Until 1967 most American states, and the federal government, occasionally inflicted the penalty of death—by hanging, by electrocution, by gas, or by shooting—for a small number of offenses, chiefly murder, but with rape an important addition in some states,[1] and with a few other offenses included here and there. I say "occasionally" because, in the half-dozen or so years preceding 1967, the penalty of death was actually inflicted, in America, on an average of some twenty-four persons annually, out of a very much larger number who had committed offenses for which death was a possible penalty. Of those actually convicted of such offenses, the large majority escaped, through jury discretion or through clemency—the latter exercised either by state governors or by special boards set up by the law of the particular state. It is quite certain, though in the nature of the case not formally provable, that another large group of persons, who could have been convicted of capital offenses, escaped, either through being charged with a lesser and noncapital offense, or through a jury finding of "guilty" only of the "lesser included offense"—a finding probably quite often motivated by the jury's desire to prevent infliction of the death penalty. (In case this is puzzling, let me give it more concreteness. A defendant who might have been found, on the evidence, to have killed with "malice"—a most problematic term, not

1. The Supreme Court has now held that the imposition of the death penalty for rape is violative of the "cruel and unusual punishments" clause of Amendment VIII to the Constitution.

clarified by centuries of verbal tossing about—and so to be guilty of "murder," might be allowed by the prosecutor to plead guilty to, say, "manslaughter"—roughly, for this purpose, killing without "malice"—receiving a sentence of a term of years; or a jury, even in the face of enough evidence to support a verdict of "premeditated murder," might nevertheless find the defendant guilty only of "manslaughter," so that the greatest possible punishment was imprisonment. This is permissible, and the term "lesser included offense" is used, because killing without "malice" (manslaughter) can be looked on as "included" within the offense of killing *with* "malice" (murder), being composed of all the elements of the more serious offense *except* "malice," so that in proving a case of "murder" *except* for the "malice," one will have proved "manslaughter.") Since defendants escaping death in this way are never formally identified as guilty of the capital offense, it is impossible to give numbers or percentages, but no person experienced in the field doubts that the processes I have here described have very often taken place.

By 1967, a great litigation effort was well under way, aimed at persuading the Supreme Court of the United States that the infliction of death by law violated the national Constitution—in particular the Eighth Amendment, which forbids the infliction of "cruel and unusual punishments." This and various connected questions were before the Court for a long time; meanwhile, executions were "stayed" by court order, pending outcome of the suits. No person has been executed since 1967, partly because of these stays, and partly because of stays incident to now (1974) current litigation.

In June of 1972, the Supreme Court, by a five-to-four decision in the case of Furman v. Georgia, in some sense upheld the position of those attacking capital punishment. I have to say "in some sense" because *nine* full opinions were delivered, and the opinions of the five Justices constituting the majority were not in agreement on the reasons for the decision or, by inference, on its scope as a precedent for the future. Two Justices in the majority of five would have held capital punishment to be wholly forbidden by the Constitution, as a "cruel and unusual" punishment in itself. The other three, with some variation in reasons and in expression, seemed to be holding that capital punishment *as currently administered* violated the Constitution, because of the arbitrary selection of a small number of sufferers—a selection mostly made not on clearly articulated grounds but on the basis of a standardless "discretion" lodged in juries and judges.

It would be a task of great complexity, probably not ultimately eventuating in a clear picture, to try to analyze all these opinions or to place their reasonings into harmony with other quite recent Supreme Court case-law developed by the capital punishment litigation. For purposes of the present historical sketch, it would seem to be enough to say that the decisive ground of the 1972 Furman case's anti-capital punishment ruling—the ground persuasive to the marginal Justices needed for a majority—was that, out of a large number of persons "eligible" in law for the punishment of death, a few were selected as if at random, by no stated (or perhaps statable) criteria, while all the rest suffered the lesser penalty of imprisonment.

Through the operation of causes which those of us who oppose capital punishment can only guess at, the country did not sigh with relief at the Court's having taken on itself the burden of eliminating this vestigial cruelty, bringing the United States into line with most civilized nations. Instead, a good many of the state legislatures went zealously to work, drafting and passing statutes which, it was hoped, would get around the Supreme Court decision and make it possible once more to inflict the death penalty. These statutes—and pending bills—approach this work in two principal ways. Either the death penalty is made "mandatory" for certain offenses, or there is promulgated a set of what purport to be "standards" for guidance of the selection (usually by juries) of those who are to die.

New litigation is now in progress challenging the constitutionality of these statutes.[2] The focus of this book will not be on constitutional questions as such, but on the standardlessness and mistake-proneness of the process by which people are chosen to die, even after the passage of these new laws, and on the unacceptability of this system to us as citizens, quite apart from the question of its constitutional vulnerability.

2. The fate of this litigation is described and discussed in the first piece in Part II, *infra*, pp. 135 ff.

Chapter *2*

Mistake and Arbitrariness—An Overview

I HAVE SAID that the central thesis of this book is that the problems of mistake and caprice are ineradicable in the administration of the death penalty. In a narrow sense, then, I am saying that these seemingly more "precise" statutes, just referred to, do not cure the fundamental defect that was the basis of the Supreme Court's 1972 decision in the Furman case, outlawing capital punishment as it has been administered. Though the truth of this assertion can be established from the new statutes alone (see Chapter 7), I want to make my case in a wider frame of reference. This widening will consist in opening to the reader's view the entire *series of decisions* made by the legal system as a person goes the road from freedom to the electric chair. Let us take an overview of these.

I will skip over the preliminary decision on arrest, and go on to the two-pronged decision made by the prosecutor. On the facts before him, he must first decide whether to *charge* an offense carrying the penalty of death, or a lesser offense. If he decides to charge the capital offense, he must quite commonly decide whether to *accept a plea of guilty* to a lesser (and therefore noncapital) offense, thus permitting the defendant to escape at this early stage the possibility of execution, at the price of going to prison without trial. (Now it is quite true that a grand jury often plays a part in the making of the first of these decisions—the decision on what to charge—but grand juries are commonly quite heavily under the influence of the prosecutor; in any case, the decision as to the nature of the charge brought must be made by somebody, and it will be immaterial to any of the discussion in the rest of this book whether this decision be made by the prosecutor alone or by the prosecutor in co-action with a grand jury. For this reason, and for simplicity's sake, I will from now on refer to this choice as one made by the prosecutor.)

If the *prosecutor,* having charged a capital crime, is nevertheless willing to accept a plea of guilty to a lesser offense, then the *defendant* has in turn the choice of accepting or rejecting this offer. This dreadful choice has to be made by a man in custody, often disoriented and frightened, and hence dependent upon advice, and susceptible to following possibly bad advice; at this point, then, the choice is partly or wholly made by the *lawyer* for the defendant. With the best of intentions, this lawyer's decision is often a difficult one. (The "plea bargain" will be more fully explained in Chapter 5.)

If a "plea bargain" is not struck, then the defendant goes on trial for his life. At the end of this trial, the jury has a number of decisions or choices to make, most of them veiled by the secrecy of the jury-room. It must decide what the gross *physical* facts were: Did this defendant, for example, actually stab the deceased, or did somebody else do it? Did the defendant stab the victim at a time when the victim was trying to stab the defendant, or did he stab a man whose knife was sheathed? (I will now mention, not for the last time, that "mistake" as to these questions of physical fact seems to be what most people mean when they speak of "mistake" in criminal proceedings; I hope I shall be able to convince you that the range of possible "mistake" is much broader than that.) Having satisfied its mind as to the *physical* facts, the jury must then tackle the *psychological* facts. Did the defendant, who clearly (or admittedly) shot a man while that man was reaching for his handkerchief, *believe* that that man was reaching for a gun, or is the pretense that he so believed mere sham? Did the defendant *plan* this killing, or was it done in the heat of passion? Did he *intend* to kill at all?

The jury in a criminal case does not announce its decision on each of such points one by one. It simply comes in with a verdict of "not guilty," or "guilty of murder in the first degree," or of "manslaughter," or of some other offense known to the state's law. There is no question in the mind of anybody who has dealt with the criminal-law system that a jury sometimes comes in with a verdict of "guilty" of some offense lesser than the one strictly warranted by the evidence. All kinds of factors—sympathy, doubt of physical "guilt" in the narrow sense, doubt as to the other, less tangible factors going to make up "guilt," a feeling that extenuating circumstances exist, and so on—may motivate this behavior. But the pragmatic fact, visible from the outside, is that the jury, in finding a defendant guilty, let us say, of "second-degree" rather than of "first-degree" murder, is, for whatever reason and on whatever basis, *choosing* that this defendant not suffer death.

Very commonly, at this stage, the jury must rule on the "insanity defense." I single it out for special emphasis because it is so crucially important, particularly in cases of a revolting sort, likely to inflame a jury, and also because it plumbs the whole theory of criminal responsibility. A verdict of "not guilty by reason of insanity" is a jury's choice for some form of imprisonment rather than for death. (At two other points "sanity" is a critical issue. Before the trial, a court may have to decide whether a defendant is sane enough, at that time, to be tried, and, at least theoretically, it must be decided, at the time of execution, that the defendant is sane enough to be executed (a quite puzzling concept); but the sanity question of greatest importance, by far, is the question of sanity that goes to the issue of guilt of the charged crime—sanity, that is, at the time the act was committed.)

If the jury, accepting the prosecutor's version of the facts and rejecting all defenses, convicts the defendant of an offense for which the death penalty is possible, the choice then has to be made as to *sentencing*. Under the old system, condemned in the 1972 Furman case, the usual procedure was for the jury, "in its discretion," to decide whether a death sentence was to be imposed. The form of words varied from state to state; sometimes the death sentence followed automatically unless the jury recommended mercy, while sometimes the affirmative recommendation of the jury was necessary for the sentence of death. Sometimes, indeed, the judge rather than the jury exercised this "discretion." In the newer statutes referred to in Chapter 1 (the statutes designed to get around the 1972 Furman case) a *second* hearing on sentencing often occurs, at the end of which, on the basis of mitigating or aggravating circumstances named in the new law, the sentence of death may or may not be imposed. In this initial survey, it is enough to note that this choice must usually be made. (Sometimes the sentence of death is "mandatory" on conviction of certain crimes—but note, above, that prosecutor and jury practically always retain control (by discretion in charging and in accepting a "plea," and by finding the defendant guilty of a less-than-capital offense) over the decision whether conviction of this "mandatorily" capital crime can occur.)

After conviction, sentencing, and appeal, we reach the possibility of executive clemency, or clemency exercised by a pardon board. In no state, as far as I know, is it the case that a death sentence, once imposed, *must* be carried out, without the possibility of there intervening an act of mercy by some authority. The national Constitution fixes this principle for federal crime, by giving the pardoning power to the President.

Now that is about the range, though some minor points may have been skipped, for later filling in. It becomes plainly visible that the choice of death as the penalty is the result not of just *one* choice—that of the trial judge or jury, dealt with in the Furman case—but of a *number* of choices, starting with the prosecutor's choice of a charge, and ending with the choice of the authority—the governor or a board—charged with the administration of clemency.

Regarding *each* of these choices, through all the range, one of two things, or perhaps both, may be true.

First, the choice made may be a *mistaken* one. The defendant may not have committed the act of which he is found guilty; the factors which ought properly to induce a prosecutor to accept a plea to a lesser offense may have been present, though he refused to do so; the defendant may have been "insane" in the way the law requires for exculpation, though the jury found that he was not. And so on.

Secondly, there may either be no legal standards governing the making of the choice, or the standards verbally set up by the legal system for the making of the choice may be so vague, at least in part of their range, as to be only *apparent* standards, in truth furnishing no direction and leaving the actual choice quite arbitrary.

These two possibilities have an interesting (and, in the circumstances, tragic) relationship. The concept of *mistake* fades out as the *standard* grows more and more vague and unintelligible. There is no vagueness problem about the question "Did Y hit Z on the head with a piece of pipe?" It is, for just that reason, easily possible to conceive of what it means to be "mistaken" in answering this question; one is "mistaken" if one answers it "yes" when in fact Y did not hit Z with the pipe. It is even fairly clear what it means to be "mistaken" in answering the question "Did Y *intend* to kill Z?" Conscious intents are facts; the difference here really is that, for obvious reasons, *mistake is more likely* in the second case than in the first, for it is hard or impossible to be confident of coming down on the right side of a question about past psychological fact.

It is very different when one comes to the question, "Was the action of which the defendant was found guilty performed in such a manner as to evidence an 'abandoned and malignant heart'?" (This phrase figures importantly in homicide law.) This question has the same grammatical form as a clearcut factual question; actually, through a considerable part of its range, it is not at all clear what it means. It sets up, in this range, not a standard but a *pseudo-standard.* One cannot, strictly speaking, be mistaken in answering it, at least within a considerable range, because to be mistaken is to be on the wrong side of a line, and there is no real line here. But that, in turn, means that the "test" may often be no test at all, but merely an invitation to arbitrariness and passion, or even to the influence of dark unconscious factors.

"Mistake" and "arbitrariness" therefore are reciprocally related. As a purported "test" becomes less and less intelligible, and hence more and more a cloak for arbitrariness, "mistake" becomes less and less possible— not, let it be strongly emphasized, because of any certainty of one's being right, but for the exactly contrary reason that there is no "right" or "wrong" discernible.

Sometimes, there is a puzzling intermediate or hybrid case, where the "test," though expressed in exceedingly obscure language, may, in some metaphysical sense, have "meaning," so that one can, in theory, be right or wrong in some application of it. But so obscurely expressed a standard *invites* mistake, even if the standard itself, in some ideal sense, is meaningful. The truth is that we mortals cannot really tell whether such obscurely expressed standards have, in some arcane sense, any meaning, so we don't know whether, in trying to apply them, we are behaving quite arbitrarily or are making all the mistakes that are inevitable when the standards given us are all but totally unclear in expression. (I am inclined to think that this is about where we stand on the "insanity" test; see Chapter 6.)

All of this sounds uncomfortably close to philosophy, and is not the kind of thing congenial to me or, I dare say, to most of you. I have one excuse for taking you through such dull stuff, and for having the nerve to insist that you must try to follow it, going back and reading it over if necessary. My excuse I urge as clearly sufficient, for it is no less than the fact that, within a year or two, several hundred men and women may have electric current passed through their bodies until their eyeballs pop out and their brains are cooked, as a result of choices made under standards vulnerable to the objections I have just rehearsed. Let us understand these issues. Let us spare ourselves no pain of consideration before we see that occur—before we commit our society yet again to the policy of officially sanctioned killing.

For it is my assertion in this book that, in one way or another, the official choices—by prosecutors, judges, juries, and governors—that divide those who are to die from those who are to live are on the whole not made, and cannot be made, under standards that are consistently meaningful and clear, but that they are often made, and in the foreseeable future will continue often to be made, under no standards at all or under pseudo-standards without discoverable meaning. My further (and closely connected) assertion is that *mistake* in these choices is fated to occur.

At this early stage, I will anticipate only one objection—indeed, I am probably not anticipating, for it will doubtless already have arisen in your mind. Are not all human choices, including, particularly and most relevantly, all choices regarding criminal punishment, vulnerable to just these same objections?

The general answer must be "Of course they are; that is our predicament." (For a possible reservation, which I shall not try to argue, see the parenthetical paragraph ending Chapter 4.) I must therefore, to make my case, sustain the thesis that death is different—that the infliction of death by official choice ought to require a higher degree of clarity and precision in the governing standards than we can practicably require of all choices, even of choices for punishment. At this point I simply note that I take on myself that obligation and will try to redeem it in Chapter 4.

Chapter 3

Other Arguments about Capital Punishment

THE PURPOSE of this chapter is not to argue each issue in the capital punishment controversy, but rather to place the main thesis of the book, as it has just been stated, in relation to other issues in that controversy.

Let us take just the two main arguments commonly advanced in favor of the punishment of death—*retribution* and *deterrence*.

I know no way, finally, of effecting a meeting of minds, through reason, on the question whether sheer retribution is a worthy motive for action by the political society. I have never been able to get beyond the point of seeing here one of those ultimate clashes of value which cannot be resolved by argument. I am revolted by the idea of retribution through officially imposed death, just as I am revolted by the idea of poisoning for money; in neither case, in the end, am I able to *prove* to another person that

that person ought also to be revolted by either of these ideas or by both of them.

I do think, however, that those who believe in retribution as being in itself a valid ground for capital punishment may want to reexamine this belief if they are convinced that the thesis of this book is right. That thesis is that the penalty of death cannot be imposed, given the limitations of our minds and institutions, without considerable measures both of arbitrariness and of mistake. If this thesis is right, then in the full context the retribution question takes on what seems to me a new form. One must now ask oneself whether the moral value of sheer retribution is sufficient to justify not only the infliction of death in accordance with clear standards and without error, but also the infliction of death without clear standards and by mistake. No one can establish by proof that an affirmative answer to the altered question is wrong; perhaps it may be thought that, in the moral order, the exaction of vengeance is so indispensable a good that one must continue to exact vengeance even though one has faced the fact that this exaction is sometimes irrational and sometimes positively mistaken. I confess I cannot conceive the psychological possibility of such a conclusion, on the part of a normal person, but that is different from being able to prove it is wrong. As to the retribution value, then, what the thesis of this book does, if it is a true thesis, is to change the frame of reference in which the decision about the suitableness of the retribution motive must be made.

The other (and in modern days more accepted) argument for capital punishment is that it *deters* certain highly undesirable conduct. Here I think the thesis of this book has something to contribute on a logical or rational level.

It would be well first to recapitulate, without anything like full argument, the present state of the "deterrence" controversy.

First, it must be noted that what we are talking about is *not* whether the threat of punishment deters people from crime. The question, much more specific than that, is whether the threat of *death* is of significantly greater deterrent force than the threat of *long imprisonment*. How does this question now stand?

I think the answer has to be that, after all possible inquiry, including the probing of all possible methods of inquiry, we do not know, and for systematic and easily visible reasons cannot know, what the truth about this "deterrent" effect may be. We know that, on raw data, there has been somewhat more homicide in capital punishment states than in non-capital punishment states. But we cannot draw any valid conclusions from this, for factors other than the punishment system may easily explain the difference. The general problem that blocks knowledge here is that no adequately controlled experiment or observation is possible or (so far as we can see) ever will be possible. We have to use uncontrolled data from society itself, outside any laboratory. When we do that, there are two basic modes of procedure. One can compare, say, homicide statistics in states that, respectively, have or do not have capital punishment, over the same period of time. Or one can compare homicide rates in the same state, before and after the abolition or reinstitution of capital punishment.

The inescapable flaw is, of course, that social conditions in any state are not constant through time, and that social conditions are not the same in any two states. If an effect were observed (and the observed effects, one way or another, are not large) then one could not at all tell whether any of this effect is attributable to the presence or absence of capital punishment. A "scientific"—that is to say, a soundly based—conclusion is simply impossible, and no methodological path out of this tangle suggests itself. When I last sampled this enormous literature, I found two scholars were arguing over where the "burden of proof" lay—whether, that is to say, the man who asserts that capital punishment deters has to prove this proposition or lose out, or whether the man who asserts that it does *not* deter has to prove *this* proposition or lose out. When you observe that an argument is in that posture, you can be very sure that neither side has a convincing case. Nobody is arguing about where the "burden of proof" lies with respect to the assertion that families of five with incomes under $4000 are on the whole less well nourished than those with incomes over $20,000.

Nor does "common sense" help. In the first place, one of the soundest maxims of "common sense" is that one is to look for and respect *evidence,* acknowledging as unsolved those problems which the best evidence leaves unsolved. "Common sense," moreover, has little to say about the state of mind of people meditating murder or rape; you or I' might think the chance of death would "deter" us more than would the chance of imprisonment—but neither I nor most of my readers have ever seriously meditated murder or rape, and in fact we have no basis for a "common sense" judgment in this matter.

To go into deeper but still charted water, suicide is one of the half-dozen chief killers in the United States, ranking up somewhere near heart disease and automobile accidents. If tens on tens of thousands of people want, or think they want, to die, how unlikely is it that some of them—disturbed as most of them are—might, consciously or unconsciously, pick the commission of a capital crime as a means of suicide? (It often doesn't work, but that is true of all kinds of suicide attempts.) The possibility cannot be dismissed that capital punishment may in this way stimulate homicide. We just don't know.[1]

On all scores, then, the "deterrence" question is wide open and will, as far as anyone can see, remain wide open indefinitely. The connection with the thesis of this book is clear. If this thesis—that we do not and cannot administer the penalty of death without arbitrariness and mistake—is true, some might think we ought nevertheless to go on administering it if there were a clear case for its saving innocent lives by deterring homicide. There is, however, no case for the proposition that any such effect is to be attributed to capital punishment. We are entirely free to abolish capital punishment on the ground that it is not and cannot be rationally administered, without any fear, or at least any fear warranted by proof or experience, that any innocent life would thereby be endangered.

When we turn from the two usual arguments in *favor* of capital punishment—retribution and deterrence—to the other side, we find, above all, that the *cruelty* of it is what its opponents hate—the cruelty of death, the cruelty of the manner of death, the cruelty of waiting for death, and the cruelty to the innocent persons attached by affection to the condemned—unless, of course, he has no relatives and no friends, a fairly common condition on death row. (I do not intend to broach at this point the question whether, as a matter of *law*, death is a "cruel and unusual punishment" within the meaning of the Eighth Amendment to the national Constitution; whatever the answer to that question may be, no sane person can doubt that the agony of waiting and of execution is cruel in the

1. A student of mine, Robert Krakower, Yale Law School 1982, has summarized the state of this question in a paper.

colloquial sense.) Here again, the connection with the thesis of this book is clear. One might decide (though I never could) that the infliction of this suffering is justified when it is inflicted on the *right* person—the person selected by the invariant and correct application of *clear* standards, set up by society through its constitutional forms. It would, I think, take a much hardier mind to conclude that this suffering may legitimately or desirably be inflicted on the basis of *unclear* standards, or no standards, with mistake, in the long run, a certainty. And it must be added that cruelty itself is greater when the arbitrariness or the mistake is visible to the condemned person, as must sometimes be the case. To sum up, if the nature of our institutions—and, indeed, of any institutions we can project—is such that the choice for death must often be standardless or mistaken, then the retribution question, the deterrence question, and the cruelty question all take on a different form and must be rethought. Is retribution a moral imperative when it is to fall on some persons arbitrarily chosen or chosen by mistake? Are we justified in using "deterrence" as an excuse for the execution of some persons chosen arbitrarily or by mistake when there is no affirmative case whatever for the reality of the "deterrence" effect?[2] Are

2. The chief development on the deterrence question, since the above passage first appeared, has been the publication of the work of Isaac Ehrlich, and the scholarly reaction thereto. Ehrlich attempted to show, by advanced mathematical methods, the positive deterrent effect of the death penalty. Many social scientists of standing have maintained that this objective was not attained; Professor Daniel Glaser usefully summarizes the work of these people in a 1979 article.

In 1978, in a report titled *Deterrence and Incapacitation*, a distinguished panel set up by the National Research Council not only reached the conclusion that Ehrlich's work had itself produced "no useful evidence" on the deterrent effect of the death penalty, but went further and committed itself to the opinion that usable evidence concerning this deterrent effect is in all probability never going to be produced. This seems to lead back around to the very same position as was taken in the text of this book, in its first edition.

we justified in inflicting very great suffering when that suffering is to fall on some persons chosen arbitrarily or by mistake? If the thesis of this book is right, then those are the forms that must be taken by the three cardinal questions about capital punishment. I submit that every member of our society lies under the moral duty of deciding whether I am right in the contention that capital punishment cannot be administered without arbitrariness and mistake—and under the duty, if I am judged to be right in this, of rethinking each of the above three questions in the light of this thesis.

Chapter *4*

The Problem of Other Forms of Punishment

STARTING with the next chapter, I shall take up one by one the steps at which choice is made for death or life, and I shall try to show that each of these steps contains—and must contain—a component of arbitrariness and a potentiality for mistake unacceptable in a decision for the death of a person. I have already mentioned, though very briefly, that much the same things could be said of the very same steps when the decision made, say, is between five years and ten years in the penitentiary—when the decision, that is to say, has in any way to do with the quantity and kind of punishment or indeed with the question whether punishment shall be imposed at all. Since I have neither hope nor desire of persuading you that criminal punishment ought not to be administered at all, and since it is my thesis that there ineradicably inheres in our system an arbitrariness and a susceptibility to mistake which is absolutely unacceptable where the punishment is death, I must (as I said at the end of Chapter 2) take on the task of persuading you that death is different—that we ought not to accept, with respect to the death penalty, the arbitrariness and fallibility in decision which we must accept, and no doubt will go on accepting, with regard to other punishment. (This is not to say that I am entirely happy with the degree of standardless discretion and fallibility in decision which mark the administration of punishment less than death, but that is another matter, of much greater complexity, perhaps to be taken up at another time.)

Is death different? Are there grounds for requiring, as to the death penalty, greater certainty, both in standards and of correctness, than as to other penalties? I shall first discuss this question as a question of policy and then try to show that our legal system has in fact responded by accepting, in many ways, the specialness of death and the appropriateness of requiring, for death, more careful procedures than for any lesser punishment.

Plainly, any civilized system of punishments has to rank some punishments as more severe than others. It is very hard to conceive of any system in which this distinction is not felt and followed. Sometimes the distinction is very plain because it is a purely quantitative distinction, on a single scale; ten years in prison is a more severe punishment than sixty days in jail; a ten-dollar fine is a less severe punishment than a ten-thousand-dollar fine. Sometimes the distinction is qualitative, and hence a little harder to handle. Generally, in our culture, imprisonment is considered more severe than a fine. It might be questioned whether a ten-day jail sentence is a more or a less severe punishment than a ten-thousand-dollar fine, and the answer might well vary with the circumstances of the defendant, but the question is a real one.

Where does death stand on this scale, or on this set of scales? I should have thought that our culture had committed itself beyond doubt, and in the most unequivocal manner, to the proposition that death is a far more severe penalty than imprisonment. This is confirmed from every side. The penalty of death is reserved for the most serious and detested crimes. "Commutation" always means the commuting of a death sentence to a prison sentence; we would think someone had taken leave of his senses who spoke of the "commutation" of a prison sentence to a death sentence or who could, for example, use the term "recommendation of mercy" to mean recommendation of death instead of prison. A Stoic philosopher might want to argue this point, but we are dealing with a real system in the real world; grades of severity have to be judged, in such a frame, as they are judged by the culture in which they exist, and few things are clearer than the fact that our culture sees death as more severe than imprisonment, by an order-of-magnitude jump. This is confirmed by everything from the most famous soliloquy in Hamlet to the desperate battle of condemned people to be allowed to live in prison rather than to be put to death.

To the uniqueness of extinction, to the uniqueness of the agony of anticipating extinction, to death's unique destruction of all hope, must be added, when we are talking about death as a socially chosen punishment, the uniquely irrevocable character of killing. It is of course true that in some sense (as Bernard Shaw, I believe, pointed out) imprisonment is irrevocable. Everything that is done or suffered is irrevocable; even a day's happiness is irrevocable. But it is a blurred vision indeed that cannot see a radically different *kind* of irrevocability in death. Time spent in prison through mistake cannot be given back *in specie,* but some compensation can be attempted, as the law attempts it for many wrongs, all of them "irrevocable" in the same sense as that in which imprisonment is irrevocable. A prison sentence may be shortened if the behavior of the prisoner seems to warrant this, or if cooled judgment makes the originally awarded sentence seem too harsh. Prison itself may furnish some opportunities for choice and some chance (as Camus has so perceptively remarked) for the criminal's making amends. If a wrong determination on "sanity" seems to have been made, a prisoner may be transferred to medical facilities. Some or all prisoners may have some hope of betterment in the conditions under which they must live. Imprisonment, then, though very bitter, and though irrevocable in the same sense as are all other sufferings and even happenings, offers many chances for change, many windows of hope.

Having seen this, we can see at once that death *is* different, that it is irrevocable in quite a distinct sense from the general irrevocability of all happenings. If a mistake of any kind is discovered, it is too late. In every way and for every purpose, it is too late.

Now to the second step: Ought higher standards of clarity and certainty in administration to be required for the imposing of severer penalties?

Here again, the consensus of civilization seems clear. Parking tickets have to be disposed of summarily; practically speaking, you just pay the man the two dollars and fight the charge only if you want to make some kind of point. The imposition of a ten-day jail sentence obviously

does not call for the kind of "due process' that ought to be
furnished when what is in question is a ten-year prison
sentence. If death, as the culture unambiguously
assumes, is by far the worst punishment, then the
requirements of "due process" for death may reasonably
be set higher than the requirements of "due process" for
other punishments.

All this would seem fairly obvious, and I rehearse it
all because even the obvious ought not to be left unsaid
when it is a step in an argument about killing, and because
it is essential that I meet squarely the objection that all I
have to say about arbitrariness and mistake in a death case
is true as to all decision.

As irrefutable confirmation of all the above, we ought
now to note that the strictly legal side of our culture has
taken abundant note of the differentness of death as a
punishment and of the consequent differentness of "due
process" requirements when death is the stake in play; the
relevance of legal provisions here is that they authoritatively establish our collective judgment on this question.

Our legal system is simply saturated, at all levels, with
the ideas that requirements of fairness, certainty, and so
on—all the things we mean when we say "due process of
law"—vary with the seriousness of the interest at stake,
and that, as a corollary, imposition of the penalty of death
carries with it a more exacting requirement than other
punitive action of the political society. As to the first of
these ideas, the Supreme Court, as recently as 1972, has
remarked: "It has been said so often by this Court and
others as not to require citation of authority that due
process is flexible and calls for such procedural protection
as the particular situation demands."

But of course practice throughout the country and
the world has always illustrated this obvious truth. No

traffic court affords the kind of "due process" that is given the felony defendant. No procedure for fixing a real property tax assessment has the safeguards that surround a proceeding that may result in the loss of one's home.

We are here interested mostly in the recognition, by our own legal system, of the heightened "due process" requirements that move into place *when life is at stake.* All the state legal systems in one way or another—by requiring jury unanimity, by forbidding pleas of guilty to a capital offense, by providing for automatic appeals, and so on—have recognized this distinction, quite without compulsion from the national Supreme Court. But when such compulsion was needed it has been forthcoming. For many years our federal Supreme Court required of the states that they invariably assign counsel in capital cases, while leaving the question of counsel in noncapital cases open to variation based on special circumstances; the fact that at last the Court decided counsel should be required in all serious criminal cases does not impair the force of the earlier cases as establishing national recognition of the immense difference between imprisonment and death. On the other side of the coin, the Supreme Court has several times upheld, as not violating any federal guarantee, state laws imposing more stringent requirements for trial in capital cases than in other cases.

The late Mr. Justice Frankfurter, in a concurring opinion, once said:

These cases involve the validity of procedural conditions for determining the commission of a crime in fact punishable by death. The taking of life is irrevocable. It is in capital cases especially that the balance of conflicting interests must be weighted most heavily in favor of the procedural safeguards of the Bill of Rights.

The late Mr. Justice Harlan, concurring in the same case, said:

So far as capital cases are concerned, I think they stand on quite a different footing than other offenses. In such cases the law is especially sensitive to demands for that procedural fairness which inheres in a civilian trial where the judge and trier of fact are not responsive to the command of the convening authority. I do not concede that whatever process is "due" an offender faced with a fine or a prison sentence necessarily satisfies the requirements of the Constitution in a capital case.

I have quoted from these two Justices because they, perhaps more than any others in the last few decades, represent a principled conservatism in respect of the function of the Supreme Court in reviewing state criminal cases—and they were both exceedingly learned and astute lawyers. A distinction to which they so unequivocally committed themselves can hardly need further validation.

Now let me wrap this chapter up by reminding you how all this ties in with the main thesis of the book. That thesis is that our criminal-justice concepts and institutions cannot administer the punishment of death without a measure of arbitrariness, and a measure of susceptibility to mistake, unacceptable when life or death is the issue. A possible major objection to this thesis would be that this arbitrariness, and this susceptibility to mistake, are just as great when imprisonment, and not death, is the stake, and that we cannot consistently, therefore, use this arbitrariness and mistake-proneness of the system to cause us to hold our hand on killing, since the very same considerations ought to cause us to hold our hand on *any* punishment—a result nobody now, if ever, realistically could advocate. The answer this chapter gives is, first, that the most obvious common sense would counsel that certainty and fixity of standards is more stringently requisite as penalties grow more serious; secondly, that our culture has for centuries unambiguously, and with good reason, looked on death as a more serious penalty than imprisonment; thirdly, that our legal system has—as a matter of practice and as a matter of constitutional law—committed itself to this distinction. We ought, I should suppose, to try to improve as much as we can the administration of *any* punishment. But we need not fear that we will have committed ourselves to the Utopian dream of a world without any criminal justice if we conclude that our system of administering criminal justice simply will not decently do as a system for separating out those who are to die.

Let us go on, then, to consider the stages of decision, from freedom on the street to the electric chair, and ask ourselves whether each of these stages is or can be made free enough from arbitrariness and error to make us willing to ordain that some shall be killed at the end of this terrible series of choice.

(I have chosen not to argue in this chapter the possibility that the life-or-death decision, because of the emotion that swirls around it, and because of the perhaps unique difficulty of putting into clear words the concepts that are to govern the life-or-death choice, may really be *more* mistake-prone and *less* amenable to rational standardization than decisions made in other parts of the criminal law. I avoid this argument, though I think there may be much in it, because it cannot be made without some appeal to intuition. What has been said quite suffices for sustaining the burden this chapter takes on.)

Chapter 5

The Decisions on Charging and on Plea-Bargaining

WHEN WE LOOK at criminal justice as a *process* rather than as a set of rules associating certain punishments with certain crimes, the concept of rigorously mandatory linkage between act and punishment fades out. It begins to fade when we consider the process of *charging*. How and by whom is it decided what crime to charge, after the raw factual picture—or, more accurately, the raw evidence, in hand and anticipated—is digested in part and in part forecasted?

The rough answer (not subject to sufficient qualification to make analysis of the qualifications here worthwhile) is that the *prosecutor* makes this decision, and that his decision is within large limits "discretion-

ary"—subject to no clearly statable rule, but formed, even
by the most conscientious of prosecutors, on the basis of
an open-ended series of factors, such as an estimate of
difficulties of proof or a belief that a charge of the
maximum offense that might be proved would result in an
unduly severe punishment given the circumstances, and
so on. It is the ". . . and so on" that is most important, for
there is no rule to bar entry of any noncorrupt
consideration—and the occasional entry of a corrupt
consideration is exceedingly hard to establish. The
United States Court of Appeals for the Fifth Circuit, in a
widely approved case, has said, "The discretionary power
. . . in determining whether a prosecution shall be
commenced or maintained may well depend upon
matters of policy wholly apart from any question of
probable cause." [United States v. Cox, 342 F. 2d 167, 171
(5th Cir.) *certiorari denied,* 381 U.S. 926] A *fortiori,* the
decision as to what charge to bring is likewise discretionary.

I am not going to come down very hard on this stage
of the process, because its part in administering the death
penalty in the future, if that penalty is reinstated, is hard
to predict. Probably up to now it has not played much part
in capital cases; these are all very serious, and the
tendency has been to charge the maximum offense, since
leniency might be anticipated further down the line. On
the other hand, we are told by a leading authority on the
"charging" decision (Miller) that (as we easily might
guess) one of the standard uses of "discretion" in charging
is the avoidance of "punishment harm that administrative
officials regard as too severe . . . because conviction of
the maximum offense carries a statutory mandatory
minimum sentence. . . ." Now some of the new
death-penalty statutes do seek to make capital punish-

ment mandatory for certain described offenses; it would seem anticipatable then, that the discretionary power to charge a lesser offense would sometimes be used to avoid this severe result. If a bill in a certain state, for example, becomes law, death by hanging will be *mandatory* for one who "*recklessly* causes the death of a law enforcement officer, Corrections employee or fireman while such officer is in the lawful performance of his duties. . . ." Is it necessary to construct an elaborate hypothetical case to convince anybody that the killing of a policeman, in line of duty, not by intention but merely "recklessly," might sometimes occur in such a way that it would be simply absurd, as well as incredibly cruel, to *hang* the "reckless" person? I would think it inevitable that, with such statutes in force, many cases must occur wherein conduct, though plainly falling within the statutory language, and plainly deserving punishment, equally plainly could hardly be seen by a sane person as deserving death. It would seem nearly inevitable, then, that prosecutors would use some common sense in charging, just as they now do with respect to offenses carrying minimum terms of imprisonment. But that "common sense," however much we might applaud its exercise in the individual case, is subject to no rule of law, but is exercised "arbitrarily," on the basis of "discretion" alone. Nor can this practicably be changed, for change would require the condition, contrary to fact and to possibility, that we know in advance of trial, or even of charge, of what offense the accused person is actually guilty.

Let me go just a little further into this (even though the "charging" choice may not be of cardinal importance) because it is in a way paradigmatic of a problem that entirely pervades any attempt to take "discretion"—which always to some extent covers arbitrariness—out of criminal law. The only tool available for doing this is the *verbal* description of some course of conduct, and the rigorous association, with conduct fitting that form of words, of a fixed (or minimum) penalty. And the invariant truth is that no verbal description ever succeeds in anticipating all the special (and often highly important) variations in circumstances that may occur. I remember discussing with some lawmakers a proposed statute which would impose a *mandatory* sentence of twenty years on something called "hijacking" an airplane. I cannot quote this proposed law exactly, but it defined this crime, approximately, as "using force, or the threat of force, to cause any person lawfully in possession and control of an aircraft to divert that aircraft to any destination other than the one intended and desired by such person in lawful control and possession," and for doing that you *had* to get twenty years. That sounds just right if you happen to be thinking (as most people then were thinking) of the well-publicized cases of hijacking of passenger jets for political purposes. But I interposed the question, "What about a guest in his friend's Piper Cub, owned and piloted by the friend, who says 'I've got a girl I want to see in Akron, and if you don't put this thing down there, I'll beat you up when we land'?" Punishment? Of course; you can't fool around with airplanes. But *twenty years?* I never found anybody who thought that would be right.

We are dealing with something eternal, or at least humanly eternal. It passes the wit of man to anticipate all circumstances in drawing a law—even all those circumstances which would make application of the law, as drawn, ridiculous. If strictly mandatory death-penalty statutes are enacted, the law will give somewhere; one of the places where it *can* give is at the stage of *charging*, and I would expect to see many cases of prosecutors' charging less than they might have proved, to avoid the danger of this most drastic of sentences. But those decisions are not subject to any rule, and cannot—for the reason given above—practicably be made subject to any rule.

The part that will be played in future by prosecutors' unbridled "discretion" in charging is, as I hope I have candidly indicated, conjectural (though not, I think, beyond probable conjecture). The next (and closely associated) stage—that of "plea-bargaining"—is not conjectural. By far the majority of our criminal cases are handled by plea-bargaining. TV shows, where the case goes to a hard-fought trial, don't perhaps instruct us adequately on this, but everybody knows about it down at the courthouse. What is plea-bargaining?

At the conclusion of the "charging" process, just discussed, a defendant stands accused of one or more crimes, and if no intermediate process intervenes he will go on trial for those crimes. For simplicity, let us use just one—say, "assault with a deadly weapon." On TV, the next step is the trial. At the real courthouse, in a very large percentage of the cases, the next step is a bargaining session or sessions between the prosecutor (or an assistant) and the defendant's lawyer. As in the "charging" process, the prosecutor's bargaining stance is conditioned by an open-ended series of factors—the likelihood of winning on the serious charge already filed, the tax on the trial resources of the county, the defendant's prior "respectability" (a term I am not making up but am taking from a principal authority on the subject), political pressure, and so forth. The decision to offer a "plea" to the defendant—to let him plead guilty to a lesser offense than the one charged (maybe "simple assault" in the example given) and so reduce the possible punishment—is thus made without obedience to statable rule. It is made, in fact, on the basis of just that kind of ruleless "discretion" that the Furman case seemed to be condemning when the life-or-death choice was made by a jury.

Yet this is one of the critical (and almost always exceedingly important) official choices between life and death, made on the defendant's way from the street to the electric chair. And it is utterly visionary to think it can be eliminated or reduced to rule. Our entire criminal-law system lives and moves and has its being in the "plea-bargaining" institution. An impossible tax would be placed on our resources if we had to hold full trials for all the people who now are induced to plead guilty, by a promise of what is in effect a limitation on possible punishment.

Nor is there any practicable way to reduce this process to rule. Just as with the "charging" process, reduction to rule of the "plea-bargaining" process would require the impossible—an *adjudication* of the exact degree of guilt of the defendant, in advance of trial, or, as a rather inefficient and quite problematic alternative, forcing the prosecutor to go to trial in every case on the maximum charge barely suggested by the known evidence, without regard to his own estimate of the probabilities of conviction. And either of these "rules," besides being absurd and productive of needless harm, would tax our resources beyond any point our society will possibly stand for.

So, within any foreseeable future, one of the absolutely crucial decisions for life or death—the decision whether to offer the defendant a chance to plead guilty to a noncapital offense—will be made administratively, on the basis of administrative discretion, without clear standards in law.

This is emphatically not to say that these decisions

either have been or will be in the main corrupt or tricky. (Nor can it be said, people being what they are, that some of them will not be corrupt—motivated, for example, by political considerations or by the state of public feeling as to certain crimes.) Rulelessness is something different from corruptness. But rulelessness will not do for what is probably the most widely significant choice separating the doomed from those who must go to prison.

There is in this process, too, the possibility of mistake. For example, one of the factors that commonly affect the prosecutor's bargaining stance in the "plea-bargaining" process is the defendant's prior record in the broadest sense—not only his prior convictions but also suspicions, associations, and the like. Since no procedure of any kind is prescribed for the ascertainment or assessment of this material, mistake is easily possible.

But this kind of mistake is not the most serious fault with plea-bargaining in the death-penalty case. The most serious is that, inevitably, some are spared while others are pushed on along the road to execution, without any *rule* to govern the choice—only such prudential and rough-equity considerations as may move the particular prosecutor.

One ought not to finish on plea-bargaining without mentioning the role of the *defendant's* lawyer. The person in custody accused of capital crime is very likely to be frightened and not in any shape to know what is best for him. More often than not, he does not at all understand the criminal justice system. (These facts, as if they needed it, have received confirmation in many judgments of the Supreme Court.) He is thus heavily dependent on the advice of his lawyer—often an assigned counsel or an overworked public defender. This lawyer too, having no clear guides in the form of rules, and required to assess a situation in a hurry, may make a mistake, and if his mistake consists in advising his client not to accept the chance to plead guilty to a noncapital offense, this may be the really relevant choice for death made at this stage. I would estimate, however, that the prosecutor's choice whether or not to offer such a chance is far more often the significant one.

(One truly parenthetical but very important point ought to be added about the connection of plea-bargaining with capital punishment. In a case that by any stretch of evidence and imagination might be capital, the threat of the death penalty, even as a bare possibility, puts in the prosecutor's hand, as he bargains, a counter of something like infinite weight, often virtually forcing the defendant to plead guilty to something, even though the chances may be great that he would have been acquitted—and virtually forcing his lawyer to advise him to plead, lest he himself, the lawyer, be responsible for his client's execution. Indeed, in view of the very small number of persons actually executed in recent times (some two dozen people a year, before the "stays" described in Chapter 1 took hold) it is a not unreasonable conjecture that these people died, in great part, *pour encourager les autres* to plead guilty to a lesser offense than capital, without invariable regard to provable guilt. I do not think this a desirable thing, but I drop it here, for it is not connected with my principal thesis.[1])

---

1. Some of the concrete realities of plea-bargaining, in a single death case, are brought out in the second piece in Part II, *infra*, pp. 135 ff.

Chapter 6

The Trial and Verdict

IF THE DEFENDANT has been charged with a capital offense, and if no plea-bargain has been arranged, then he goes on trial for his life, usually before a jury. That jury will have at least one, and usually two, things to determine. First, it must determine whether (*and of what*) the defendant is guilty. Secondly, if it finds the defendant guilty of a crime which *may* be punishable by death, it must, under many of the new death-penalty statutes now being enacted in the states, determine whether the penalty is to be death or life imprisonment. This chapter will deal with the first of these functions—the "guilty or not-guilty" function. The next chapter will take up the sentence-choice function.

The "guilty or not-guilty" function of the jury has two aspects, though they are in practice inseparable. In a capital case, the jury must determine whether the defendant is guilty of the capital offense—punishable by death—with which he is charged. But in very many cases its finding of "not guilty" of the capital offense may be accompanied by a finding of "guilty" of some "lesser offense." Let us again get this concept clear. If one person kills another person and is charged with willful murder, a jury may well find that he indeed killed the other man but did so recklessly without "willfulness." In such a case, under proper instructions from the judge, the jury may find the man "not guilty" of murder but nevertheless "guilty" of "negligent homicide" or "manslaughter." (Both the terminology and the exact rules will vary from state to state, but some such set of possibilities exists in every state.)

Pragmatically, what this means is that a jury can very considerably manipulate penalties; it is very often not faced by the choice of either freeing the defendant or convicting him on the capital charge. Ideally, the jury makes this choice solely on the basis of the "facts"; in the case put, it simply registers, by its verdict, its conclusion on the factual question, "Was this killing 'deliberate' or was it simply 'reckless'?" But there are two enormous flaws in this neat picture. First, the "factual" question (like the one in the example) may be exceedingly difficult to determine by evidence; this means, obviously, that mistake is easily possible. Secondly, there is in actual practice no way to keep a jury from finding a defendant "not guilty" on the capital charge but "guilty" of the lesser included offense, whatever its secret views may be on the actual facts; indeed, the law usually gives juries great latitude on this. If we add into all this the natural human tendency to see facts and to evaluate evidence in a manner leading to a desired conclusion, it becomes, to say the very least, easily possible that the jury, which on this matter is practically uncontrollable, may find any defendant "not guilty" on the capital but "guilty" on the lesser charge, on the basis of whatever it may regard— whether humanely or corruptly—as circumstances in mitigation, or even on the basis of appealing personal characteristics in the defendant. This result, like the decision of the prosecutor to accept a plea of guilty in the plea-bargaining process, sounds good; somebody escapes death. The trouble is that if you turn the coin around, somebody else *suffers* death because the jury did *not* find him guilty of a lesser offense rather than of the capital charge. And if the jury's *milder* verdict may be a function of its sympathies, then its *sterner* verdict, by inevitable logic, may be a function of its *lack* of sympathy. And it must be remembered that this alternative, open to the jury, is not effectively controllable, but may mask any amount of purely "discretionary" decision. In the nature of the case it is not possible to say how often this happens; we have no independent procedure for determining whether the jury was *factually* right. But I do not know anybody familiar with the process who thinks the possibility I have here sketched not a genuine one, often realized in fact.[1]

But, for simplicity, let us turn back to that aspect of the jury's work which consists in the simple determination of "guilty" or "not guilty" on the capital charge. The performance of this task carries with it two principal problems. First, the determination of questions of sheer fact is not easy; mistake is bound to occur now and then in the long run. Secondly, the *definitions* of capitally punishable murder often employ verbiage and concepts exceedingly difficult to explain and apply.

As to the first of these difficulties, it is enough to say

---

1. The Supreme Court has now distinctly recognized this; see *infra*, pp. 122 ff.

that juries, at best and even ideally, are not infallible; to be fallible means to *make a mistake* sometimes. A very important addition is the reminder that the questions of sheer *fact* which a jury must determine in a capital case extend over a range both enormously wider and far more difficult than the question "Did the defendant kill the deceased?" I must emphasize this again and again. In the movies and in the press, "mistake" seems usually to mean "The jury found that he did it, but now it turns out that it was done not by him but by somebody else." Even on the level of sheer mistake as to physical fact, the array of possible errors is enormously more extended than this. The first piece of paper that happened to catch my eye on my desk as I was writing the above sentence contained a digest of an Arizona case in which the critical question was not whether the defendant shot the deceased, which was conceded, but whether the deceased threatened the defendant with a knife, so that the shooting was in self-defense. Since, it seems, only the two of them were present, the evidence consisted only of the defendant's own testimony, plus the reputation of the deceased for carrying a knife, and the finding of a knife—which finding, incidentally, had in the actual case *been concealed* by the prosecutor! Quite obviously, a jury can easily make a mistake in a case of that sort. It can even more easily make a mistake as to the endless questions of "state of mind" and "intention" which it must find on.

But the possibility of mistake in the "guilty" or "not guilty" choice does not end with mistake either as to physical or unproblematically describable psychological fact. The jury is also called upon to pronounce upon mixed questions of fact and law, questions that have puzzled the most astute legal minds. One of these, perennially with us, is "premeditation." "Premeditation" is very often a defining characteristic of capital murder. If "meditation" connotes some duration of thought, then "premeditation" might be expected to denote thought about the killing over a considerable time. But judges have repeatedly said that the premediation need not be of any particular length; a moment is enough. On the other hand, "premeditation" is not the same as "intent to kill."

If you try to run down, in standard treatises or in the cases, the distinctions in state of mind required for the different "degrees" of murder or for distinguishing between the traditional offenses of "murder" and "manslaughter," the first thing you find is that the solution of the exceedingly difficult psychological problems involved varies from state to state. You also find that the "definitions" proffered are intelligible enough when extreme examples are used; it is easy to see that a long-planned poisoning for the sake of insurance money is "premeditated," while a killing in the very first flare of passion on discovering one's spouse in bed with somebody else is probably not "premeditated"—though, on the basis of some doctrine, it could be. The difficulty of course occurs in the close cases which actually come to court in great number. We are told, for example, that "premeditation" requires no particular duration of time, yet that frequently the line of demarcation between first and second degree murder is drawn by putting into the second-degree class (not punishable by death) *intentional* killings without "premeditation." We are invited to distinguish between "murder" and "manslaughter" by reference to "greater" or "less" *measures* of passion. (How do you measure passion?) The statutes and the literature abound in such archaic terms as "affray" or "lying in wait." In sum, in a great many close cases, no matter how patiently the judge tries to explain to the jury that which he himself only cloudily understands, the net result must be that twelve laypersons have no alternative to using their general sense of the equities of the matter. But this means that these purported rules, at the crucial line of separation between those who are to die and those who are to live, conceal a discretion which, however benevolent, is to all intents and purposes standardless.

But the most crucial point is reached when we get to the "insanity" problem. In every state, in some manner, "insanity" is a defense to a charge of capital (or indeed other) crime. If the defendant can satisfy the jury that his act bore some legally defined relation to "insanity" as the law defines it, he escapes conviction—usually facing compulsory hospitalization instead—hospitalization that is often not much, if any, more desirable than prison.

There have been three major approaches by law to the "insanity" problem: the so-called "M'Naghten" rule, the "irresistible impulse" rule, and the recent "Durham" rule. (The first and third are named after the cases in which they were enunciated. The Durham rule has not won any acceptance.)

The M'Naghten rule says that one is relieved of criminal responsibility if, as a result of "disease of the mind" he does not "know the nature and quality of the act" or, "if he did know it . . . he did not know he was doing what was wrong." Every word in this rule, except the prepositions and definite articles, has been problematical. Dean Abraham Goldstein, one of the greatest living authorities on the subject, says, for example, that the "word 'know' has been at the center of the controversy. . . ." Does it mean "formal cognition" or "emotional awareness"? How about "wrong"? Does it mean "morally wrong" or "legally wrong"? Dean Goldstein says that the "word is generally given to the jury without explanation."

And so on. (Dean Goldstein, incidentally, makes a brilliant and in my view irrefutable case for the proposition that the M'Naghten rule need not have had the constricting effect on the "insanity defense" that has been given it. But I do not understand him to say that it can be made into a precise instrument for separating those who should be held responsible from those who should not—still less for separating those who are to live from those who are to die.)

The second "rule" is the rule of the "irresistible impulse." Here again we run into a deep philosophic problem. To the determinist, all "impulses"—indeed all urges eventuating in action, whether "sudden" or not—are "irresistible"; this is shown by the fact that they were not resisted, for to the determinist that which happens is that which must happen, through the working of antecedent causes. Since this won't do, where do we draw the line? No change in verbal form can get around the central problem, and no satisfactory way has ever been devised of communicating to the jury the meaning of a standard carrying about with it this basic philosophic difficulty.

Thirdly, the originally much-acclaimed "Durham" rule, announced for the District of Columbia in 1954, not generally adopted elsewhere, and now abandoned even in the District, uses the word "product" as the key verbal symbol: Was the act the "product" of "mental disease" or "mental defect"? But the cause-and-effect relationship contained in the word "product" is utterly ambiguous, and "mental disease" is, as Dean Goldstein points out, an exceedingly problematic concept.

Probably in part as a result of the ferment caused by the putting forward of the Durham rule, later attempts have been made, notably by the American Law Institute, to put words together that will communicate to a jury, for guidance of its action, a satisfactory "insanity" test. All this effort may very well have resulted (or may promise to result) in there reaching the jury more and better testimony on "insanity," and on the jury's working within a freer range in using this testimony. But few now pretend—and the pretense fades as knowledge grows—that any "rule" is or can be without a very substantial component of "discretion." This, like "mercy," sounds good, unless you are on the wrong end of it. "Discretion," in that case, means that you are being executed without at all knowing why—and to the rest of us it means that we are executing people without being able to say clearly why we picked just these people to execute. On the whole, I find no reason to modify what I said several years ago in the Morris Ames Soper Lecture at the University of Maryland:

We are committed, as a society, not to execute people whose action is attributable to what we call "insanity" or who are mentally incapable of standing trial, or who are what we call "insane" at the time of execution. As to the second and third of these, little need be said. In judging a defendant's capacity to participate effectively at his trial, we take into account neither low intelligence, unless, perhaps, he is clinically an imbecile, nor cultural inaccessibility, to him, of any understanding of the proceedings, just as we disregard his lack of financial resources to engage able counsel or to set afoot investigation that might clear him. As to insanity at the time of execution, this is so familiar a phenomenon in fact, and the procedure for ascertaining and acting upon it is generally so defective, that the thing speaks for itself. Obviously, mistake is easily possible in either of these two respects, and doubtless often occurs. Let me focus on so-called "insanity" as a defense.

Once again, let us remember that we have committed ourselves not to kill by law, or even to punish, anyone who satisfies certain criteria as to the connection of "insanity" with the commission of the act. Yet the astounding fact is that, having made this commitment, for what must be the most imperative moral reasons, we cannot state these criteria in any understandable form, in any form satisfying to the relevant specialists or comprehensible to either judge or jury, despite repeated and earnest trials. The upshot of the best writing on the subject is that we have so far failed in defining exculpatory "insanity," and that success is nowhere in sight. Yet we have to assume, unless the whole thing has been a solemn frolic, that we execute some people, and put others into medical custody, because we think that the ones we execute fall on one side of this line, and the others on the other side.

I am talking about mistake, and it is hard to apply the concept of *mistake,* of rightness or wrongness, to the application of criteria of the quality we have succeeded in expressing, criteria which we do not ourselves even pretend to understand. But what a fearful alternative faces us here! Either mistake is possible as to the application of such criteria, and therefore extremely likely to occur, given the quality of the criteria, or else the criteria themselves are quite meaningless, and mark no line. If the latter is true, then we are executing some people, and treating others medically, on an irrational basis.

It would not be surprising if this were so, for we are dealing here, in truth, with philosophic issues which philosophy has quite failed to resolve—issues of determinism, free will, and responsibility. But we are not debating these issues philosophically. We are putting some humans through inutterable agony on the basis of a pretense, nothing short of frivolous, that we have satisfactorily resolved these issues. How can we dare go on doing this?

I want now to digress, briefly, to cover a special problem which seems to fit here better than anywhere else. As I have worked on this lecture, I have, of course, talked it over with many people. I want to mention now one particular view which I have encountered several times. I have heard it said, by people I must respect, that they generally deplore the use of capital punishment, as to almost all killings—the *crime passionel,* the street-fight knifing, or even the fatal mugging for money—but that they believe a few crimes—the Sharon Tate murders, for example, or the multiple mad killings by Starkweather—to be so horrible as suitably to be atoned only by death. I introduce this special view at this very point in order to focus attention on the fact that it is precisely as to such crimes that we run the greatest chance of misapplication of the insanity "test" to which we must be taken solemnly to have committed ourselves. This is true, above all, for an intrinsic and inescapable reason. Where the killing is of a kind colloquially describable as mad, and actually is so described in newspaper headlines, where the crime exhibits a total wild departure from normality, we come exactly to the point where consideration of the insanity problem is at once most necessary and most difficult. The man who kills his wife's lover in a fit of rage is not necessarily mad at all. To call sane the man who, for no visible reason, walks into a barber shop with a Tommy gun and shoots a dozen barbers and customers, is to call into question our deepest assumptions as to what sanity, in social life, can possibly mean. We must, in such a case, face the issue of exculpatory insanity. But I have already reminded you that the tools we have elaborated for resolving it are about as useful as flamingoes are for playing croquet. In every case, therefore, of the supremely revolting murder, we face in particularly acute form the exculpatory insanity question, without adequate means, to say the very least, for answering it. How likely is it that we will answer it rightly? Before we frame our reply to that question, we have to face the further realistic fact that the issue of "insanity" is referred, with inadequate if not totally meaningless directions, to people who must, if they are normal, view the defendant with extremest abhorrence. I suggest that those people who disapprove of the death penalty in general, but who would apply it in such cases, ponder these facts.

(I should point out here, parenthetically, that it is only with respect to the punishment of death that our insane "insanity" rules do major damage. If a "sane" man is mistakenly classified as "insane," and confined indefinitely in a state hospital, then that is in itself a very heavy punishment. If an "insane" man is mistakenly classified as "sane," and sentenced to that indefinite imprisonment we call "life," then his condition can be, and is, reviewed medically from time to time, and he may be, and sometimes is, transferred to a hospital. The difference is of an altogether different order of magnitude from the difference between killing and not killing. I hope, also parenthetically, that I will not be taken to have implied that people like Starkweather could ever safely be turned loose, under any foreseeable state of the art of psychiatry.)

I would only draw the reader's attention to the last paragraph of this quotation. The "insanity" problem is a problem in prudent management from time to time, *until* we hit the death-penalty case. At that point the "insanity" problem changes character altogether and goes to the heart of our moral order.

Now I think I have said enough to show that the first verdict, the verdict that says "guilty" or "not guilty," and if "guilty" then "guilty of what," is arrived at by a process which invites and requires, at some points, the use of standardless discretion, however camouflaged, and which also is, at many points, susceptible of mistake— either mistake of fact or mistake in the application of standards (or pseudo-standards) to fact. This is not surprising. It would be very surprising if it were not so; modern insights into law have made it very plain that most if not all law has these characteristics. What is surprising is that we go on executing people as a consequence of the outcome of such a process, once we have seen into it.

Let us pass on to the second stage under many of the new capital-punishment statutes—the stage of explicit choice between death and imprisonment.

Chapter 7

The Sentence-Choice

THE MINIMUM MEANING of the 1972 Furman case (often referred to above) which declared unconstitutional the administration of capital punishment as up to then carried out, probably can be read (if one attends principally to the reasoning in the opinions of Stewart and White, the marginal Justices) as a condemnation of standardless discretion in *sentencing*—a discretion often lodged in the jury or judge. In the end, I hope to have convinced the reader that standardless discretion, as well as mistake-proneness, are not to be found only at the sentencing stage but permeate the whole series of choices that have to be made on the way from street to gallows; at least one more, "clemency," remains for the chapter after this. But it was natural for the states desiring somehow to retain capital punishment to try so to react as to answer specifically this objection of standardlessness in the jury's choice of sentence.

Reaction has taken two forms. In some states, the death penalty has been made mandatory for certain crimes; this entirely removes the "jury discretion" objection but of course does not alter any of the other difficulties heretofore discussed or the "clemency" difficulty discussed in the next chapter. With these newly "mandatory" states may be grouped those states continuing to seek to enforce capital punishment under "mandatory" statutes antedating the 1972 Furman case. (We may throw in here the odd case of North Carolina, where, over vigorous dissent, a bare majority of the state Supreme Court held that the Furman case had no other effect than to abolish the jury's power to recommend mercy, so that the penalty of death became mandatory in cases where it had previously been subject to jury reduction; this odd reasoning explains the grisly fact that there were at last count *forty persons* (twenty-five of them black) on death row in North Carolina alone, out of 114 in the nation—more than a third, in a state not at all known for its savagery.)

In some other states, a new stage in the process has been added, in an attempt to meet the Furman case's objection. (A few states already had this second stage.) After conviction of a capital felony, a second hearing is held, at the conclusion of which the jury (or the judge) decides between life and death. This decision is to be made, under these statutes, on the basis of certain "standards," and we can appraise the efficacy with which they meet the Furman case's objection, as I have interpreted that objection in the first paragraph of this chapter.

Let's look at the statute from Texas, here reproduced in its entirety, from the Texas Code of Criminal Procedure; I earnestly ask you to work through it with me, checking my back- and cross-references; they are not difficult—merely tedious—and perhaps the tedium will be relieved if you keep in mind what is at stake:

Art. 37.071.   Procedure in capital case
(a) Upon a finding that the defendant is guilty of a capital offense, the court shall conduct a separate sentencing proceeding to determine whether the defendant shall be sentenced to death or life imprisonment. The proceeding shall be conducted in the trial court before the trial jury as soon as practicable. In the proceeding, evidence may be presented as to any matter that the court deems relevant to sentence. This subsection shall not be construed to authorize the introduction of any evidence secured in violation of the Constitution of the United States or of the State of Texas. The state and the defendant or his counsel shall be permitted to present argument for or against sentence of death.
(b) On conclusion of the presentation of the evidence, the court shall submit the following issues to the jury:
(1) whether the conduct of the defendant that caused the death of the deceased was committed deliberately and with the reasonable expectation that the death of the deceased or another would result;
(2) whether there is a probability that the defendant would commit criminal acts of violence that would constitute a continuing threat to society; and
(3) if raised by the evidence, whether the conduct of the defendant in killing the deceased was unreasonable in response to the provocation, if any, by the deceased.
(c) The state must prove each issue submitted beyond a reasonable doubt, and the jury shall return a special verdict of "yes" or "no" on each issue submitted.
(d) The court shall charge the jury that:
(1) it may not answer any issue "yes" unless it agrees unanimously; and
(2) it may not answer any issue "no" unless 10 or more jurors agree.
(e) If the jury returns an affirmative finding on each issue submitted under this article, the court shall sentence the

defendant to death. If the jury returns a negative finding on any issue submitted under this article, the court shall sentence the defendant to confinement in the Texas Department of Corrections for life.

(f) The judgment of conviction and sentence of death shall be subject to automatic review by the Court of Criminal Appeals within 60 days after certification by the sentencing court of the entire record unless time is extended an additional period not to exceed 30 days by the Court of Criminal Appeals for good cause shown. Such review by the Court of Crminal Appeals shall have priority over all other cases, and shall be heard in accordance with rules promulgated by the Court of Criminal Appeals.

Added by Acts 1973, 63rd Leg., p. 1125, ch. 426, art. 3, § 1, eff. June 14, 1973.

Now first of all we can disregard, as not relevant to the questions opened by this book, the purely *procedural* provisions of this Article, except to note that while the jury is held to "finding" on three "issues" only, "the court" (i.e., the judge) may admit in evidence "any matter" he "deems relevant to sentence"—a somewhat puzzling contradiction. (I should say once and for all, however, that intricacy of procedure, and even *purely procedural* "fairness," are no substitute for *standards*.) Let us rather concentrate on the three *issues* on which the jury must "find," listed in subsection (b) just above.

The first "issue," in subsection (b)(1), is really puzzling. Texas, in its Penal Code, defines "murder" as follows:

§ 19.02. Murder
    (a) A person commits an offense if he:
    (1) *intentionally or knowingly causes the death* of an individual;
    (2) intends to cause serious bodily injury and commits an act clearly dangerous to human life that causes the death of an individual; or

(3) commits or attempts to commit a felony other than voluntary or involuntary manslaughter, and in the course of and in furtherance of the commission or attempt, or in immediate flight from the commission or attempt, he commits or attempts to commit an act clearly dangerous to human life that causes the death of an individual.

(b) An offense under this section is a felony of the first degree.

Amended by Acts 1973, 63rd Leg., p. 1123, ch. 426, art. 2 § 1, eff. Jan. 1, 1974. [Emphasis added.]

"Capital murder," in turn, is defined as follows:

§ 19.03. Capital Murder

(a) A person commits an offense *if he commits murder as defined under Section 19.02(a)(1)* of this code and:

(1) the person murders a peace officer or fireman who is acting in the lawful discharge of an official duty and who the person knows is a peace officer or fireman;

(2) the person intentionally commits the murder in the course of committing or attempting to commit kidnapping, burglary, robbery, aggravated rape, or arson;

(3) the person commits the murder for remuneration or the promise of remuneration or employs another to commit the murder for remuneration or the promise of remuneration;

(4) the person commits the murder while escaping or attempting to escape from a penal institution; or

(5) the person, while incarcerated in a penal institution, murders another who is employed in the operation of the penal institution.

(b) An offense under this section is a capital felony.

(c) If the jury does not find beyond a reasonable doubt that the defendant is guilty of an offense under this section, he may be convicted of murder or of any other lesser included offense.

Amended by Acts 1973, 63rd Leg., p. 1123, ch. 426, art. 2, § 1, eff. Jan. 1, 1974. [Emphasis added.]

Remember that this whole sentencing procedure applies only to persons *already found guilty* of "capital murder." Now since a "capital" murder, as § 19.03 (just quoted) says, must be a murder of the §19.02(a)(1) sort, where the defendant (see above) *"intentionally or knowingly"* causes the death (go back and check this if in doubt) then it seems certain that a jury, having found that the defendant "intentionally or knowingly" caused the death, *must already have found in the affirmative* on the *first* "sentencing" issue—the issue framed by Article 37.01(b)(1). Again, go back and check if in doubt. At the very best, the difference between "intentionally and knowingly" (§19.02(a)(1))on the one hand, and on the other "deliberately and with the reasonable expectation that the death . . . would result" (Article 37.071(b)(1)) cannot possibly be anything but totally puzzling to a jury, as it is to me, and as I am sure it is to you.

The *third* issue (Article 37.07(b)(3) above) is also quite puzzling. In the Texas Penal Code, "voluntary manslaughter," *not* a capital offense, is defined as follows:

§ 19.04. **Voluntary Manslaughter**

(a) A person commits an offense if he causes the death of an individual under circumstances that would constitute murder under Section 19.02 of this code, except that he caused the death under the immediate influence of *sudden passion arising from an adequate cause.*

(b) "Sudden passion" means passion directly caused by and arising out of provocation by the individual killed or another acting with the person killed which passion arises at the time of the offense and is not solely the result of former provocation.

(c) *"Adequate cause" means cause that would commonly produce a degree of anger, rage, resentment, or terror in a person of ordinary temper, sufficient to render the mind incapable of cool reflection.*

(d) An offense under this section is a felony of the second degree.

Amended by Acts 1973, 63rd Leg., p. 1123, ch. 426, art. 2, § 1, eff. Jan. 1, 1974. [Emphasis added.]

You can see right away, if you read the emphasized words in §19.04(c), that the jury, in deciding between "murder" and "manslaughter," and in rejecting "manslaughter" and finding the defendant guilty of "murder," has already as good as resolved in the affirmative this *third* death-penalty issue—the issue whether the conduct of the defendant in killing the deceased was an "unreasonable" "response" to "provocation" (Article 37.071 (b)(3) above). Here, again, the question of "reasonableness" of response and the question whether the "cause" of "sudden passion" was "adequate" are really the same question, or at least look so much like the same question that no jury could possibly tell the difference. Thus the *third* issue under Article 37.071(b) has, like the *first* issue thereunder, already been as good as resolved before the "sentencing" stage is reached, and the jury, as to these two issues, is called on only solemnly to repeat, in all practical effect, the findings it must have made already, when it found the defendant guilty of "capital murder" under Section 19.03.

This means that, after all, only the *second* of the three issues is actually of practical significance in fixing the life-or-death choice. Let me set it out again, to fill the cup of horror. The jury must decide:

"(2) whether there is a *probability* that the defendant would commit criminal acts of violence that would constitute a continuing threat to society;" [Emphasis added.]

People are then to live or die, in Texas, on a jury's *guess* as to their *future* conduct. (Incidentally, this is true whether or not my analysis of the other two "issues" is right, because a negative finding on the second issue precludes death—see Article 37.071(e)—whether the findings on the other issues be predetermined by the

"guilty" verdict, as I have argued, or are freshly made.)
This is really enough to stamp this section as outside the
bounds of civilized law. It seems almost supererogatory to
go further. But I must, for I want to cover the whole
ground. First, this guessing of Texas juries is to be in a
rather confined field; they are guessing *which people in
the narrow class of deliberate murderers* are likely to
commit the violent acts referred to, *in prison* or
elsewhere, many years later, if they are finally released.
Secondly, the named acts are described with double
vagueness. Hitting someone with your fist is a "criminal
act of violence"; does the section mean that a jury must
vote to electrocute persons shown to be given to fisticuffs?
If not, where is the line? Secondly, what is the difference
between "criminal acts of violence" which *do,* and those
which *do not,* "constitute a *continuing* threat to society"?
You may have an answer; I have none. But if you have an
answer, are you satisfied that an average Texas jury will
accept, understand, and follow it? Is this what they call a
standard in Texas? Not when I lived there; in those days,
they were more forthright.

Note, finally, that the jury, to support a death
sentence, must find "Yes," on each of the three "issues,"
"beyond a reasonable doubt." What on earth does it mean
to say that *"beyond a reasonable doubt"* a man will
"probably" be criminally violent? Can a jury handle a
crazy question like that? And does "a probability" mean
"some substantial chance" or "a better than even
chance"? Either usage is correct.

I picked up the statute from Texas because that
happens to be my home state; it was not selected as
conspicuously horrible. Obviously, we cannot analyze
them all. Bear with me (remembering the protruding
eyeballs) through one more of these new "standard"

statutes, again one which came to me at random, the one from Georgia. I reproduce it here from the Georgia Code, adding emphasis for clarity in the references to follow:

§ 27-2534.1 **Mitigating and aggravating circumstances; death penalty**—(a) The death penalty *may* be imposed for the offenses of aircraft hijacking or treason, in any case.

(b) In all cases of other offenses for which the death penalty may be authorized, the judge shall consider, or he shall include in his instructions to the jury for it to consider, any mitigating circumstances or aggravating circumstances otherwise authorized by law and any of the following statutory aggravating circumstances which may be supported by the evidence:

(1) The offense of murder, rape, armed robbery, or kidnapping was committed by a person with a prior record of conviction for a capital felony, or the offense of murder was committed by a person who has a *substantial* history of *serious* assaultive criminal convictions.

(2) The offense of murder, rape, armed robbery, or kidnapping was committed while the offender was engaged in the commission of another capital felony, or *aggravated battery*, or the offense of murder was committed while the offender was engaged in the commission of burglary or arson in the first degree.

(3) The offender by his act of murder, armed robbery, or kidnapping knowingly created a great risk of death to more than one person in a public place by means of a weapon or device which would normally be hazardous to the lives of more than one person.

(4) The offender committed the offense of murder for himself or another, for the purpose of receiving money or any other thing of monetary value.

(5) The murder of a judicial officer, former judicial officer, district attorney or solicitor or former district attorney or solicitor during or because of the exercise of his official duty.

(6) The offender caused or directed another to commit murder or committed murder as an agent or employee of another person.

(7) The offense of murder, rape, armed robbery, or kidnapping was *outrageously or wantonly vile, horrible or inhuman* in that it involved torture, *depravity of mind*, or an *aggravated battery* to the victim.

(8) The offense of murder was committed against any peace officer, corrections employee or fireman while engaged in the performance of his official duties.

(9) The offense of murder was committed by a person in, or who has escaped from, the lawful custody of a peace officer or place of lawful confinement.

(10) The murder was committed for the purpose of avoiding, interfering with, or preventing a lawful arrest or custody in a place of lawful confinement, of himself or another.

(c) The statutory instructions as determined by the trial judge to be warranted by the evidence shall be given in charge and in writing to the jury for its deliberation. The jury, *if its verdict be a recommendation of death*, shall designate in writing, signed by the foreman of the jury, the aggravating circumstance or circumstances which it found beyond a reasonable doubt. In non-jury cases the judge shall make such designation. Except in cases of treason or aircraft hijacking, unless at least one of the statutory aggravating circumstances enumerated in Code section 27-2534.1(b) is so found, the death penalty shall not be imposed.

One may note in passing that the death penalty *may* be imposed, apparently as a matter of sheer discretion still, for two crimes—treason and aircraft hijacking, a peculiar linkage, until one remembers who rides airplanes. In all other cases, what Georgia has done is to lay down a smokescreen of plenteous words, which, on hasty reading, mask the fact that exactly the same old unbridled jury discretion is there, if only the jury, guided by court and prosecutor, can grope its way through the verbal haze. For two things are clear.

First, a jury does not *have* to recommend death even if it finds one "aggravating circumstance," or many of these; besides, there is no review by anybody of a jury's *failure or refusal* to find an "aggravating circumstance" "beyond a reasonable doubt." Secondly, it is impossible to imagine a murder, rape, or kidnapping which cannot be described as "outrageously or wantonly vile" or evidencing "depravity of mind." How many rapes are not "wantonly vile" and "depraved"?[1] *All* murder—the willful killing of a human being without justification or even adequate provocation—is "vile" and "depraved." Perhaps a few armed robbers might escape here as a matter of law, but how many could be sure of escaping under *all* of (3), (6), and (7)?

Look at (1). What do "substantial" and "serious" mean?

The best one can say is: (1) That the jury is in *all* cases entirely free, just as before the Furman case, *not* to recommend death, no matter what it "finds"; (2) that, on the other hand, except possibly for a few cases of armed robbery, and even fewer unimaginably abnormal other cases, the jury is in fact entirely free to *recommend* death, because kidnapping, murder, and rape *always* involve at least some "depravity of mind," and other such qualities set forth in the law; (3) the listed "aggravating circumstances" are in part (and every part is vital, for only *one* need be "found" to support a death sentence) exceedingly vague.

Note, moreover, that the *judge* may instruct the jury to consider *any* mitigating or aggravating circumstances which occurs to him.

(There is another feature, funny but for grimness, in the above Georgia statute, at (b)(7). Since Georgia law defines an "aggravated battery" as a battery (i.e., attack on the person) which deprives the victim of a member, or of

---

1. Rape is no longer a permissible ground for imposition of the death penalty; see note 1 on p. 18, *supra*.

the use of a member, or disfigures him, the concept is a preposterous one when applied to murder; either it is always present in murder, which deprives the victim of the use of all his members, or else it functions absurdly as an "aggravating circumstance," since it can make little difference to a dead man whether he can lift his right leg. I mention this inclusion of "aggravated battery" as an aggravating circumstance, supposedly present in some murders but not in others, as a symptom of the hasty thoughtlessness with which some of these new state statutes have been set into place.)

No jury need be hampered by such nonstandards. The practical position remains unchanged; the Georgia jury, without real restraint and without real standards, chooses life or death.

I am sorry for administering to you this dose of technicality. But had I not done so, I hardly think you would have taken my mere word for the real character of these new state statutes, purporting to set up "standards" for the jury's choice between life and death, in response to the 1972 Furman case's condemnation of standardless "discretion" in this matter. It is very hard to believe, until one analyzes closely, that the states actually have come up with such solutions in this most serious of matters. As it is, you will have to take my word, tentatively at least, that the statutes in other states resemble the two samples given; we cannot go through them all.

The facts of the matter are clear, nationwide and in the round. The new statutes *do not effectively restrict* the discretion of juries by any real standards. They never will. No society is going to kill everybody who meets certain preset verbal requirements, put on the statute books without awareness or coverage of the infinity of special factors the real world can produce.

And let us remember again that, loose and standard-less as they are, these new statutes would bridle discretion, if they bridled it at all, at only *one* stage in a process of choices. The decision what to charge, the readiness or nonreadiness to accept a guilty plea, the jury's selection of the offense for which to convict, the decision on "insanity," the decision on "clemency"—all these choices remain (to a degree totally unacceptable for the death-choice) without real standards, or highly vulnerable to mistake, or both.

Let us recall finally, here as elsewhere throughout the whole series of life-or-death decisions, the strange reciprocal relation between "vagueness" and "mistake." "Depravity of mind," one of the Georgia sentencing criteria, may seem to you, as it does to me, a term so vague as to make the "standard" in which it occurs a nonstandard, a pseudo-standard, a phrase having the look of a standard but possessed of no resolving power. But if another view be taken—the view that "depravity of mind" *has* a real meaning in some metaphysical sphere of transcendent lexicography, so that there is drawn, in that abstract realm, a real line between "depravity" and "nondepravity"—the position is still no better. For this precise meaning, even if assumed to exist, is not discoverable by humans. If there is a line, the light is too dim for us to see it. *Mistake* is therefore exceedingly likely—indeed, quite certain—to occur frequently. It really depends on our philosophy of language whether we say that this phrase, "depravity of mind," has no sharp meaning and so cannot decently be part of a "standard" or say that it *has* a "correct" meaning, so that every presented case does in fact fall on one side or the other of a line, but that this line (and this is the empiric fact, not changeable by philosophy) is impossible to locate accurately, so that mistake in judgment is certain. There is nothing to choose between these alternatives; neither will do for hanging men and women.

Chapter *8*

After Sentencing (Appeal, Post-Conviction Remedies, Clemency)

WE HAVE NOW brought the defendant through the entire first stage of the process of conviction and sentencing to death. We have seen that this process comprises either three or four main strategic choices—the choice of the prosecutor to charge a capital crime, the choice of the prosecutor not to accept a guilty plea to a lesser crime, the jury's finding of "guilty" on the capital charge, and (except as to the crime for which death is in some states the mandatory penalty) the sentencing choice, made by judge or, more commonly, jury, for death rather than for imprisonment. I think we have been able to see that, as to each of these choices, there is a far greater than negligible chance of mistake, and a quite unacceptable level of pure "discretion," without standards in law. This latter characteristic is found almost chemically pure in the first two stages—the prosecutor's decision to charge a capital crime and his decision not to accept a plea—and this fact alone is of crushing significance, for the plea-bargaining stage is the iceberg of which the rest of the criminal law is the tip that shows. In the two later stages we have covered—conviction and sentencing—we have seen that an exceedingly broad discretion, usually lodged in the jury, is masked by formal statements defining the "elements" of the crime, and by formal "standards" for sentencing; these definitions and standards contain terms of a vagueness entirely unacceptable in regard to the infliction of death, and they are in any case not actually binding on a jury that wants to show leniency—the other side of the coin being that any jury may use them as it will for the reverse of leniency.

This adds up to a system for making choices that we ought not to accept when the result may be death. But there is more yet. In this chapter, I shall carry the system on to the end.

First, of course, is the straight appeal. An automatic appeal is usually provided when the sentence is death— one of the many clear evidences, as saw in Chapter 4 above, of the recognition by our legal system of the uniqueness of death as a punishment. On this appeal, the higher court will consider whether errors in law have been committed.

Then there are other possible post-conviction remedies—*habeas corpus* and the like—a network of bewildering technicality, involving both state and federal courts, with the pattern varying for each state court system. It would serve no purpose for us to trace these out. Probably the most important thing to remember is that rarely does an appellate court, or any court in the whole post-conviction process, review as a new matter the "findings of fact" of the trial jury; I know of no case in which any such court has reviewed the prosecutor's choice to charge a capital crime or not to accept a plea; if such cases exist, they are so excessively rare that they make next to no difference in respect of the prosecutor's free discretion. Thus the whole appellate and post-conviction process exercises little corrective function over whatever mistake-proneness and standardlessness may flaw the process through trial and sentencing.

For the most part, these appellate and other post-conviction remedies have to do with *questions of law.* Also, the pursuing of these remedies requires resources—by which I mean money, for lawyers' fees and for other purposes. In the round, then, these judicial remedies after sentencing either share the weakness of the process up through sentencing, or suggest inquiry into the weakness analyzed in Chapter 9 (*Mistake of Law),* or are made partly or wholly inaccessible, or of greatly reduced efficacy, by the want of money, a problem general considered in Chapter 10. For these reasons, I shall not spend any more words on them, but ask you to keep them in mind when considering the matters raised in Chapters 9 and 10.

After all judicial remedies are exhausted, then we move into the stage of possible clemency. In the capital case, "clemency" means, almost invariably, the change of the sentence of death to a sentence of life imprisonment or of imprisonment for a long term of years; only in the rarest of cases, where clear proof of entire innocence comes to light between trial and execution, does any condemned man go free.

As to federal crimes, the power to commute death sentences is lodged by the Constitution in the President. In the states, the power is usually in the governor, but in some states boards either have the power or play some part in its exercise.

The clemency function in capital cases, like the prosecutor's function in deciding whether to charge a capital crime, or whether to accept a plea, is wholly discretionary, bound by no standards either published or discernible. A recent and most able short description of the process. Goldbarb and Singer, *After Conviction* (1973) on pages 343–348, makes this point repeatedly and unequivocally. "*While not exhaustive,* investigative reports in capital cases are *less perfunctory* than for other clemency applications"—a damnation with faint praise if ever I saw one. "While all states publicly announce the commutation decision, only a minority of the states publicly provide the reasons for their decisions." "*While it is impossible to know* which considerations are most influential when commutation of the death sentence is at stake, several obvious factors *probably influence* the decision." After this last sentence, Goldfarb and Singer mention intoxication, provocation, duress, viciousness of the crime, the degree of society's outrage, the fairness of the trial as perceived by the clemency authority, and doubts as to the guilt of the prisoner. This listing is not presented as exhaustive, nor do these factors stand in any fixed or statable relation to result; we have simply an open-end series of commonsense factors probably going into the making of a decision that is almost as purely discretionary as one's decision as to what college one is to attend.

One man has had his death sentence commuted because he "rehabilitated himself" while awaiting execu-

tion; others, equally "rehabilitated," die. Governors
Alfred E. Smith and Herbert Lehman of New York, both
great humanitarians, commuted the sentences of all
those whose convictions the New York Court of Appeals
had upheld by a *divided* vote. One survey seems to show
that a positive recommendation of either the trial judge or
the prosecuting attorney—a recommendation altogether
discretionary and bound by no standards—is exceedingly
important. There is some indication that favorable
publicity has an effect; this is indeed almost a corollary of
the factor, mentioned above, of the degree of societal
outrage.

Some governors who wholly disbelieve in capital
punishment have commuted all death sentences. Others
of the same opinion consider it their duty to leave some
scope of operation to the state's law on the subject,
regardless of their own beliefs, and commute selectively.
Former Governor Michael V. DiSalle of Ohio, a man
whose humaneness shines in his book, *The Power of Life
or Death* (1965), seems to have been of the latter sort and,
in the book, gives us what is probably the fullest record we
have of commutation philosophy as held by a single man
who has wielded this terrible power. What appears is,
indeed, a most admirable use of discretion—"clemency"
at its best—but the book is on the other hand a thorough
documentation of the lack, in the clemency process, of
anything that could possibly be thought to approach a
standard, and a documentation, as well, of the entire
dependence of the quality of "clemency" judgments on
the personality of the official empowered.

In Connecticut, we are told by Goldfarb and Singer,
it has been the practice to schedule the commutation
hearing early on the day set for execution, and to require
the attendance of the doomed man. I suppose that if the

decision were for death, some reasons might be given, perhaps even on the spot. But those reasons could never be reasons rooted in law. For clemency knows no standards that are invocable as a matter of law. To the saved, this is mercy, of a quality not strained. To those who learn they are to die, it is irrational choice for death—the final such choice in a long series. From that point on, there is no discretion; the human race becomes a killing-machine.

Chapter 9

Mistake or Uncertainty of Law

So FAR I have dealt, at every stage, with the problems of mistake on questions of fact, and with the problem of vagueness or near-meaninglessness in the "standard" for some finding—say, the finding of "not guilty by reason of insanity," or the finding of "premeditation." The picture cannot be rounded out without some attention to still another matter, one of very great difficulty—the problem which may (depending on one's legal philosophy) be thought of as the problem of "mistake of law," or the problem of "uncertainty of law."

"Questions of law" have been looked on, classically, as questions concerning the correct *rule* to apply to facts assumed to be known; this concept has eroded in modern time, but it will still do for a first approximation. Now in the course of criminal proceedings an enormous number of *questions of law* may be decided. Was the search of the defendant's home lawful? If it was not, is it the correct rule that the evidence found must be excluded at the trial? Has the defendant a right to the assistance of counsel, paid for by the state, from the moment of arrest? May the defendant's pastor be forced to testify as to a confession made to him by the defendant? Is a prospective juror who expresses distaste for the death penalty to be dismissed? Is it unlawful for the trial judge to express or indicate his own opinion of the credibility of an "alibi" witness? Does the defendant's ninety-day period to appeal include July 4? Does the evidence support a verdict of "guilty" of "felony murder"?

Hundreds of such questions of law, great and trivial, may be raised and answered in the course of a criminal proceeding, from arrest until the final appeal in the last post-conviction proceeding. Some are obvious of answer. Some are sufficiently difficult that learned judges will disagree on them. Not only the Supreme Court of the United States but the Supreme Courts of the states may and often do divide very closely on such questions, great and small. Yet the answer to the question of law, in a capital case, may decide the issue of life or death for the defendant.

Under an older and today much weakened view of the nature of law, each such question had a "right" and a "wrong" answer; the "right law" was somehow *there*, to be discovered or found by the correct use of technical reasoning. Among some lawyers and among some other people, this is still the prevalent view—more often assumed than expressed. If it is the correct view, then the workings of the capital punishment system are connected in a simple way with the decision of questions of law. Because if there exists a correct answer to every legal question then it is perfectly plain that *mistake* is possible and must sometimes occur, just exactly as mistake is possible, and must sometimes occur, with respect to the numberless questions of *fact* which have to be decided as a person is moved along the line from freedom to execution. No one could think that courts are infallible on points of law, or believe that there are not many questions of law—including many life-and-death questions—the answer to which, even if a "correct" answer exists, is exceedingly elusive and hard to be sure of. If we had no other way of knowing this, the close votes on courts of last resort—often five to four in the national Supreme Court—would irresistibly convince us of it. (It was noted in Chapter 8 that, for just this reason, some governors have commuted *all* death sentences affirmed by a divided appellate court.) There probably is a "right" answer to the question whether there is life on Mars, but if nine equally well-accredited astronomers divided five to four on the answer, we would know with absolute sureness that the right answer was hard to find or to be confident of. (And we must not forget that there was a time when nine astronomers out of nine would have opined that the sun went around the earth.)

On this view—the older, perhaps classic view—of law, we are—just as in the case of doubtful questions of fact—executing people as a result, sometimes, of flatly mistaken determinations of law. The alternative hypothesis is judicial infallibility—even five to four or four to three infallibility—and no sane person has ever claimed infallibility for any institution except the Papacy, and that only under the most rigid rules and on the most infrequent occasions, and on the basis of an assumption of divine guidance, hardly an assumption that fits our judges.

A newer and now quite prevalent philosophy of law changes and complicates—but in no way improves—the picture. Close questions of law, under this view, have no single "correct" answer; there is no law out there somewhere, waiting to be seen clearly. The situation is, rather, that judges, using the technical resources available to them—mainly precedents, statutes, and constitutional provisions—strive for law which is not disobedient to these, and which to some extent is channeled by these. But they often find that these authoritative materials do not settle, and cannot by any logical manipulations be made to settle, the question before the court. (This, in a nutshell, is because *words*, whether in statute or constitution, do not have fixed meanings through their whole range, and because no *precedent* is ever exactly like the case at bar—to which may be added the fact that American courts are not and never have been bound to follow every precedent every time, but have always had and exercised the power occasionally to *overrule* a precedent, though the occasions on which this may properly be done are themselves not susceptible of precise definition.)

This newer philosophy of law goes on to say that, where the technical materials (precedents, statutes, constitution) do not produce a clear answer—a condition often evidenced by disagreement as to the answer among equally competent and disinterested people—then obviously, since an answer is given, *something else* produces it. This something else may be the judge's sense of policy, justice, fairness. This is undoubtedly the usual case, in overwhelming preponderance. The judge may, in obedience to the style of our law, conceal the operation of these factors from the public or, quite often, from himself, but they must be there, or disagreement on questions of law among equally learned and honest judges could not occur. Competent mathematicians do not divide five to four on a question about the topological properties of a Moebius strip; if they did (and sometimes they do so divide, for a time only, on very new questions) we others could only say, sensibly, that the answer is not yet known.

Let me give an example. In the 1940's, a man named Willie Francis was condemned to death by electrocution. He was strapped in the chair and the current was turned on, but there was a malfunction and, while he could feel the current, it did not kill or seriously hurt him. He was unstrapped and taken back to his cell, to await repair of the apparatus. There was no showing of any *intent* on the part of the state (Louisiana) authorities to inflict any needless suffering. (Willie was seventeen.)

A *habeas corpus* (see Chapter 8 above) was quickly taken out, on the proffered ground that a *second* electrocution, or attempt at electrocution, would, in co-action with the first, add up to a "cruel and un-usual punishment," within the ban of the national Constitution. This question of law reached the Supreme Court, which decided, five to four, that the Constitution was not violated. The next time, the chair worked.

Now there were good arguments here on both sides. One would have to start—as so very often—with the concession by all hands that the ratifiers of the invoked constitutional provision had no "intent" whatever, positive or negative, about this. Is an *accidentally* "cruel" punishment within the ban, particularly where the avoidance of it (by canceling the second execution attempt) is easily possible? Or is a state held only to doing its best to avoid cruelty in administration of punishment? And so on.

The view of the nature of law prevalent in modern

times would say that there is no "correct" answer,
discoverable by sound technical manipulation of given
authorities. And this seems very plain, in the very case,
and in a veritable host of other cases.

*Yet people die, as Willie Francis died, on the basis of
the courts' answering such questions as though they did
have a "correct" answer.*

At best—and, as I have indicated above, this is
usually the case—what this really means is that, in the
innumerable zones of genuine doubt as to "right" law,
judges' view of policy (not necessarily expressed) form the
decision. In this process there is inevitably, as every
serious student knows, room for working of the personal
value preferences of the judge. (Lest I be misunderstood,
let me say at once that of course no judge in the Francis
case liked double electrocution; the preferences were
partly of an institutional kind, and had in part to do with
general attitudes toward the broad or narrow interpretation of constitutional guarantees.)

As to questions of law, then, we have to sum up about
like this: If the older view of law as a fixed and preexisting
body of rules is correct, then *mistake* is plainly possible,
and in view of the very great difficulty of "finding" this
law—a difficulty irrefutably proven by chronic division of
opinion, on issue after issue, among competent and
honest lawyers and judges— *mistake* is likely to be of
frequent occurrence. If, on the other hand, the newer
philosophy of law is right, and many "close" questions
really have no answer discoverable by technical means,
then decision is being made by the operation of judges'
views (to a great extent undisclosed) on policy and
fairness—with frequent divisions of opinion, among
equally informed and intelligent professionals, as to
where good policy and fairness are to be found.

This is the system we *have* to use for legal decision; it

is bootless, therefore, to ask whether it is good enough for the decision of ordinary cases. But, as we have seen in Chapter 4, the fact that a system is good enough, or has to be accepted as good enough, for ordinary decision does not imply that it is good enough for the choice between life and death. I submit that our intellectual apparatus for making decisions on close questions of law—whether you accept the old model of law that is certain but hard to find, or the new model of law that is continually being created by whatever enlightenment the judges may possess for the time being, shaped in the large, but not compelled, by antecedent authority—I submit that this system, not of our choice but the consequence of our built-in limitations, *is not good enough* for choosing people to suffer or not to suffer a bitter and cruel death. I haven't any idea how we could make it good enough; that is not my task, for I would be against capital punishment even if judges were endowed with some unimaginable infallibility as to decisions of law.

I will close this chapter by mentioning one exceedingly disturbing aspect of the "mistake-of-law" or "uncertainty-of-law" problem. There is continual *change* in the nature of what is accepted as correct law; as I have pointed out, American courts can and do overrule their own precedents. The last seventy-five years, for example, have seen a continual shift toward our judges' finding, in the Constitution, more and more stringent guarantees of defendant's rights, and this change has been participated in by all or virtually all the Justices of our Supreme Court, though by some more whole-heartedly than by others. State courts, too, change on their holdings as to definitions of certain crimes, standards of evidence, and so on. (Of course I am not here referring to *legislative* change, but to fresh and altered perceptions of courts, without legislative intervention.)

The inevitable result (a mere obvious corollary of the uncontroverted fact of change) is that some people have in the past been convicted of crime, although, either as a matter of substance or as a matter of procedure, the law has changed so as to make improper, today, convictions obtained on the same facts or by the same procedures as those previously approved.

This raises the celebrated problem of *retroactivity*. Should a man who is in prison as a result of a 1943 trial, in which he was denied state-paid counsel, be released, or tried again, now that the Supreme Court has held counsel must be provided? Should a man convicted in 1954 on evidence not now admissible be released? Should a man now be freed who was sent to prison on the basis of a definition of the word "accessory" now rejected by the state Supreme Court?

There is no good *general* solution to this retroactivity problem, either doctrinally or practically, and I am not going to attempt one here. My point here is that, where the original proceedings were *wrong enough*, under presently accepted standards, to call for release or new trial, this is *possible* in cases of imprisonment and does sometimes occur.

There is an exceedingly interesting variation. Sometimes the former trial went wrong—badly wrong—not because a question of law was wrongly decided but because the question itself was not yet fully visible, even to lawyers. I believe the Sam Sheppard case is an instance of this. Sheppard was tried, in the early 'fifties, for the murder of his wife. His trial was conducted as a circus, with the judge as ringmaster, and with the nation's lines of mass communication locked on the sensational aspects of the story that unfolded. This, incredibly but truly, was more or less the normal way of running murder trials in those days, whenever other sensational news ran short. Sheppard was convicted of second-degree murder (obviously a compromise verdict, for the state's whole case was such as to make it first-degree murder or nothing). He went to prison. In the succeeding years, there slowly began to develop a body of judicial doctrine setting bounds on the sensationalism of murder trials. After some twelve years in prison, in this quite altered climate of opinion and doctrine, Sheppard was released by *habeas corpus*, on the ground, obviously right, that the sensational publicity surrounding his trial had made his trial unfair.

Now I don't care whether you think that a great deal of "retroactivity" of this sort is good. Hardly any reasonable person can deny that some of it is good. The clear, flagrant, and plainly harmful error of law, resulting in severe punishment, ought at least in the worst cases to be corrected, just as the plain error of crucial fact can be and ought to be corrected, however belatedly.

And the point here is, of course, that the error of law, like the error of fact, is uncorrectable, however urgently it may call for correction, after the execution of the defendant. The doctors have buried their mistake. If Sam Sheppard had been hanged, then we would have had to live morally without any possibility of undoing the work of a clearly disgraceful trial.

Mistake of law, then, can occur—or law is in close cases uncertain. One of these things is true, or both are true. When made as a result of the resolution of a genuinely close question of law, then, the choice for death runs a great risk of being either mistaken or arbitrary and standardless. This plain fact must be added to all the others, of similar form, that make our legal system not good enough to choose people to die.

Chapter 10

The Warping Effects of Race and Poverty

THERE WERE, at the last count available to me, 114 persons under sentence of death in the United States. Of these, 61, substantially more than half, were black; three were American Indians. No statistics are available to me that show it, but anyone at all familiar with the subject would know that all or almost all of the 114 are poor, at least in the frame of reference wherein the expenses of effective defense against crime are to be calculated. [1]

What does poverty mean when set against the background of the system of choices for life or death, described in the preceding chapters?

Most capital offenses are unbailable, or bail is set so high as to be absolutely inaccessible to any but the affluent. This means that in the capital case every kind of

1. Late 1980 statistics show 670 people on death row; 258 are black. On another and even more damning racial aspect of the administration of the death penalty, see the footnote at the end of this chapter.

activity outside the jail—the marshaling of testimony, the verification of facts—must be carried on by somebody other than the defendant. This means money. If I were charged with murder, and if my defense (which I myself knew to be true) were that the deceased had threatened to kill me with a knife (as in the Arizona case mentioned in Chapter 6), I would want a thorough professional investigation conducted into the habits of the deceased with respect to carrying and threatening to use knives. I would want my own people looking into the question whether a knife had been found in the vicinity, and into whatever traces might exist—such as, say, the story of a hardware-store clerk—that connected that knife with the deceased. I would want to find out as much as I could about his prior record of arrests for violent crimes, of psychiatric confinement, and so on. I would want to have located and interviewed all possible witnesses to his demeanor and words just prior to our private meeting. *Above all, I would want a lawyer—not an overworked "public defender," not "assigned counsel," but the best criminal lawyer in town*, to advise me, and to work with the detective agency employed by me, toward providing everything we needed for the best possible defense case. Are not these the very minimum requirements of prudence?

But all this costs money—lots of money. So does everything else I am about to describe. I think I could just barely raise enough money for something like a fairly adequate defense—though this would utterly ruin me (and would utterly ruin most of my readers if they were in this position) because adequate investigation and good legal counsel come very, very high. But it is all completely out of the reach of the poor. The poor man—unless some public-interest organization happens to see an important issue in his case—can no more afford a really adequate defense than he can afford a year's cruise around the world on a luxury liner. He may luck out, one way or another. But he will be very heavily handicapped from the beginning.

Now this (even at this early stage) readily transposes into the key of possible, and increasingly probable, error; if a defense cannot be presented in the best possible manner, the chances of even a valid defense's being rejected are obviously increased. To the defendant, the finding of that knife may mean the difference between life and death; to the rest of us, the defendant's not finding it may mean that the court and jury, acting for us as a society, will overrule a self-defense plea that was actually valid, and sentence to death the wrong man—a kind of moral death for all of us. But we are not ready to furnish poor defendants with really adequate resources for the development of a defense, by investigation at early stages while the trail is still warm. Even if we were, the resources in manpower do not exist. We are running a system, therefore, which from the very beginning—from the hours and days following arrest—so operates as to make it enormously more difficult for the poor to bring out all the truth than it is for the well-to-do to bring out all the truth. This is, of course, just another way of saying that both conviction and conviction by mistake are from the beginning made much more likely for the poor.

Let us pass on to plea-bargaining—the point at which most criminal cases are settled, the point at which, in possibly capital cases, the decision is made by the prosecutor whether to accept a plea of guilty to a noncapital offense or to press on, with the maximum charge, for death. One of the most careful studies I have seen of plea-bargaining, that in Donald Newman's *Conviction* (Little, Brown, 1966, pages 215–217) comes down very hard on the importance of having skillful counsel at this stage, a stage which Newman says ". . . requires no less *skillful* legal ability to evaluate alternatives than is required for other decisions where evidence and convictability are involved" [emphasis added]. I have emphasized the word "skillful" because I want to stress, yet again, that at this stage you need not just any lawyer, any overworked assistant public defender or assigned counsel, but a *skillful* lawyer, skilled in this very specialized matter, and able to give it his time and undistracted attention. To get him, you have to pay for him, and pay plenty. He is not ordinarily available to the poor. So, again, the fact of poverty makes it quite plainly more likely that, in general, the indigent will have a much slimmer chance than the well-to-do at this exceedingly significant point, where the prosecutor, by deciding whether to accept a "plea," is making the choice between life and the possibility—from this point on a substantial possibility—of death.

On to the trial. It is almost supererogatory to point out at what a disadvantage the poor person stands when this stage is reached. Part of this disadvantage has to do, again, with the *investigation* vital to development of the case. I have already alluded to this at an earlier stage, and need only add that this handicap is compounded and increased when one reaches the showdown stage of trial, where all the evidence must at last be produced if it is to have any effect. *The development of an evidentiary case costs money;* the state does not, to any adequate extent, if at all, furnish that money. Another part (and what a vital part!) of the poor man's disadvantage has to do with the *quality* of his legal representation. Good trial lawyers— skilled cross-examiners, gifted advocates—are now charging something not far from $1,000 per day of trial. But if

we are (as we certainly are) committed to using an
adversary system to get at the truth, and if we base this
adversary system squarely on the energy and skill of
lawyers, how can it possibly be that it makes no difference
whether you have a superb lawyer or a mediocre lawyer?
Nobody really believes this; we just prefer to shut our eyes
to the obvious fact that the poor man, in a capital case as
in other cases, is at a crushing disadvantage—a fact
which, from our standpoint as well as his, carries the
inevitable (but morally shocking) implication that his
execution through mistake of fact, or by the application of
"discretion," or by the jury's misunderstanding of some
cloudy concept like "premeditation" or "insanity," is
more likely than it is for the well-to-do person, who can
(by ruining himself, at least) bring it about that his case be
put to judge and jury in the most favorable light by a
lawyer talented and skilled in just that art.

The appeal stage (including all post-conviction
proceedings and motions) is more of the same. At this
point, what is needed is lawyers' skill in researching and
arguing questions of law, and above all in *spotting* these
questions. Here again, who could be so naive as to think
that it makes no difference in the result whether a
superbly gifted advocate is employed (at the high price he
commands) or, on the other hand, one has the services of
a conscientious but not superbly talented assigned
counsel or public defender? But if this difference *can*
make a difference in result, then obviously, once again,
the poor are at a heavy disadvantage.

The 1963 Supreme Court case of Gideon v.
Wainwright, holding that poor people must be provided
with counsel at state expense, may have had the
unfortunate side-effect of lulling us to sleep on this issue;
the disadvantage of the poor remains, for what is needed

is not just *any* lawyer, but a lawyer specialized and highly skilled in criminal defense. Volunteer and assigned counsel, like "public defenders," often (though not always) do a good job, but you and I know perfectly well that what we would want would be the best criminal lawyer procurable. Gideon v. Wainwright does not guarantee any particular quality of representation.

(I ought to add that lawyers' skill in spotting and arguing questions of law is also important at the *trial* stage; I have known of criminal cases which were irretrievably lost, not because there was no error of law in the trial, but because the defendant's lawyer failed to make timely objection to such error.)

Obviously, the very same points can be made as to the "sentencing" stage in some of the new statutes discussed above in Chapter 7. The *discovery and proof* of "mitigating" circumstances, and the *rebuttal* of evidence of "aggravating" circumstances, may require costly investigation. The placing of these circumstances before the jury in the most favorable light to the defendant calls for advocacy in a high range—both as to talent and as to fee.

Now we come, at last, to the stage of clemency. Insofar as the sentence-commuting authority (governor or board) tries to base its decision on some fairly definite grounds, it is again obvious that the proper presentation of these grounds, from the defendant's side, depends on investigation and advocacy of a high—and costly—order. Even the effective invocation of "discretion" is an art at which not all are equally skilled.

Now stop and consider. Can you really doubt that a process like this, from first to last, is *heavily* loaded against the poor? Could you really be surprised at finding that by far the majority of people suffering death are poor? Are

you satisfied with that? If you are not, face the fact that
there is no way to change it except to do away with the
death penalty; our society is never going to support fully
adequate defenses, all the way up, for the poor, and even
if it would there are not enough first-class lawyers to go
around; the situation would be like the one suggested
when, in an old movie, a character ran for the Senate on a
platform including the promise that every American boy
was to have an education in Harvard College.

Let me now correct one possible misapprehension. I
have not said, and do not believe, that affluent people
improperly or *corruptly* escape capital punishment. What
I have said is that they, unlike many of the poor, can have
developed, and brought before the appropriate authories,
material that may bring about decision in their favor.

Now what about blackness? Why are more than half
of the people on death row black in a country with about
eleven percent blacks?

A great deal of the explanation is contained in what
has already been written in this chapter. There is a high
correlation between blackness and poverty. But I must, to
be candid, open up another possibility—one which must
remain no more than that but which must be taken
seriously. The system I have sketched, in Chapters 5
through 8, is riddled and saturated with uncontrolled
discretion, however disguised. I am not sure we can yet
assume, after the history of three hundred years, that this
"discretion" may not be influenced (often, to be sure,
unconsciously) by race.

I will not insist on this. What I will insist on, as a
matter of common knowledge, is that where standardless
"discretion" plays a part, or where close decisions of fact
must be made on disputed evidence, or where vague and
ambiguous concepts ("premeditation," "insanity") must

be applied to concrete facts, we are one and all susceptible to the tendency to see things in a better or worse light depending on our general sympathies; we fight against this, but in the end only the self-deluding think they can wholly avoid it. If this idea is right, then there is the ever-present danger that anyone against whom, for any reason, conscious or unconscious prejudice exists will come off worse than a person against whom such feeling does not exist. And of course the *unconscious* prejudice, the prejudice one thinks one has wholly overcome, is the more dangerous.

In any case, most people on death row are black, and almost all are poor. What is *your* explanation? And can you go on living with such a system?

(I ought to remind you, again, that all these considerations apply to all infliction of punishment. I cannot think that any of us can be satisfied with this condition or cease from efforts to better it. But at the very least such a system should not be employed to select some people for the supreme agony of execution. I have already shown in Chapter 4, that by ceasing to use the system for this end we are not committing ourselves to abandoning criminal punishment altogether; in law, as in life, death is supremely different.[2])

2. New light on the racist operation of the death-penalty system is found in the totally damning statistics collected by William Bowers and Glenn Pierce. The study as I have seen it covers a number of southern states and Ohio. Except for one minor inconsistency in Georgia, the *steep descending order* of death-sentence probability is (1) Black kills white (2) White kills white (3) Black kills black (4) White kills black. A typical sequence is the Ohio pattern on criminal homicide, showing death sentence incidence as a decimal fraction of $1 = 100\%$:

Black kills white .214
White kills white .056
Black kills black .017
White kills black .000

(Continued)

That last triple-zero line is repeated again and again, through the great majority of the tables, and with substantial numbers of "white kills black" homicides. In Texas, for example, 30 blacks were killed by whites; not one white went to the death house for this. In Ohio, the corresponding numbers are 47 "white kills black" homicides, and again, not one death sentence.

In virtually all the tables, moreover, even the black who killed another black had a much better chance of escaping the death penalty than the white who killed another white. For some strange reason, killing a black is dramatically less death-worthy, under these "carefully drafted" statutes, than killing a white. By far the most death-worthy thing of all—after all the "aggravating" and "mitigating" circumstances have been "weighed"—is for a black to kill a white. And by far the least death-worthy thing, after more such fiddling about with "standards," is for a white to kill a black. But really, didn't you know that already?

Chapter **11**

A Summary—
Law New and Old

Now I have sketched a shocking picture. I know that I have not meant to mislead, and I think I have not misled; minor mistakes could hardly affect this crushing case. I will not now recapitulate in detail, but will remind you only that the decisions on charging, on acceptance of guilty plea, on determination of the offense for which conviction is warranted, on sentencing, and on clemency add up (for somewhat different reasons in each case, discussed in the chapters above) to a process containing too much chance for mistake and too much standardless "discretion" for it to be decent for us to use it any longer as a means of choosing for death. We have to keep using it as a means of choosing for other punishment, even as we slowly try to make it better, but for the death of a person it will not do, and it cannot be reformed enough to do.

Suppose all the mistake-proneness and standardlessness I have laid out, step by step, were concentrated in the decision of one man. We would regard that as so evidently intolerable as to be undiscussable. But it might be better than what we have, for responsibility would at least be fixed. All our system does is to diffuse this same responsibility nearly to the point of its elimination, so that each participant in this long process, though perhaps knowing his own conclusions to be uncertain and inadequately based on lawful standards, can comfort himself with the thought, altogether false and vain, that the lack has been made up, or will be made up, somewhere else.

How have we allowed ourselves to get here? I suggest it is because of our seeing the whole process through the medium of a radically false mythology. We tend, I believe, to think of persons' being "clearly guilty" of crimes for which they ought to die. Then some of them, by acts of pure grace, are spared—by prosecutors' discretion, by jury leniency, by clemency. After all, who can complain at not receiving a pure favor? (There is here perhaps a touch of Calvinism—but to a true Calvinist a blasphemous touch, for the "grace" comes from humans all too human.)

The trouble is that the system may just as well be viewed, and with enormously higher accuracy, if numbers count, must be viewed, as one in which a few people are selected, without adequately shown or structured reason for their being selected, to die. The inevitable corollary of sparing some people through mere grace or favor is standardless condemnation of others. The thing that ought to impress us is the standardless condemnation; we have been looking too long at its mirror image; we should take courage and turn around.

One paragraph corrective of a possible misapprehension: When I condemn our capital punishment system as intolerably mistake-prone and standardless, I do not mean in any way to suggest corruptness or cruelty on the part of those who work it. The prosecutor *must* accept some pleas and reject others; I have no reason to think that most prosecutors do not try to exercise this function in a commonsense and humane manner. Juries *must* pronounce on the questions put them; if they are asked whether a particular murderer or rapist was "depraved" or "not depraved," they have to answer as best they can; if they are given an unintelligible "sanity" question to answer, they must do their best. Judges must pronounce on questions of law, whatever they may know as to their own fallibility. I have already given illustrations of the humane use of the clemency power by governors. All this is not to say, of course, that there are not some hanging prosecutors, hanging juries, hanging judges, and hanging governors. But, overwhelmingly, the trouble is not in the people but in the system—or nonsystem.

Now I have not bothered you with constitutional law. All the arguments I have put forward, without a single exception, would support the abolition of the death penalty even if there were no Constitution of the United States. But lawyers among my readers will readily see that, all the while, I have been arguing a Fourteenth Amendment case too; I have argued that there is not enough "due process of *law*" in our system to make it an acceptable instrument for the "deprivation of life." And I have here emphasized the word *law* because it is the most important word in the phrase. Good *procedure* is not enough; the bedrock guarantee is that nothing will be done to anyone without an adequate *law* that commands it—a law, I think I am warranted in saying, whose required clarity is a function of the gravity of the thing being done, as I have argued at length in Chapter 4 above.

I have not so clearly argued an Eighth Amendment case, condemning the death penalty as "cruel and unusual." But I think such a case is implied in what I have said. Probably an accurate partial gloss on "unusual" would be "not of regular or predictable incidence." And I should think the psychological cruelty of death by the human killing-machine would be greatly heightened by the victim's awareness—not from reading this book but from knowing what crimes were committed by people playing ball out there in the exercise yard—that he has been chosen without solid reason in law for the difference in treatment.

But this book is for the laity, and I quickly retire from the constitutional arena. I will close with a story about a development in the law of another time and place.

The Law of Moses is full of the death penalty. But as time went on the court in ancient Jerusalem, without of course touching one syllable of this Law, devised *procedural* safeguards so refined, so difficult of satisfying, that the penalty of death could only very rarely be exacted. So approved was this process that it is said in the Talmud that when one rabbi called "destructive" a Sanhedrin that imposed one death sentence in seven years, another said, "Once in seventy years," and two others said that, had they been on that great Court, no death sentence would ever have been carried out.

Now I used to think, superficially, that what this story meant was that the ancient Jews, abhorring the infliction of death, seized on a purely collateral and accidental means—complication of procedural safeguards—to avoid its infliction, just as the English judges of about 1800, administering capital punishment for some 250 crimes, became terribly fussy about the exact wording of indictments. And I thought the quoted remark of the two rabbis merely expressed dissatisfaction with that lack of ingenuity which had resulted in some cases' slipping through the procedural net.

As I have looked at our own system for administering capital punishment, and as I contemplate the entire insufficiency of its remotely possible improvements, I think I see a different and infinitely profounder point in the story. At this level of profundity, "procedure" and "substance" lock and become one.

I think the rabbis, in surrounding the punishment of death with nearly unsatisfiable *procedural* safeguards, were groping (or perhaps consciously moving) toward a truth reached by the quoted remark of the two last mentioned. To put it in terms they might naturally have used, I think they were saying at last, "Though the justice of God may indeed ordain that some should die, the justice of man is altogether and always insufficient for saying who these may be."

I suppose, really, that is what this book is about.

Part II: The Newer Phase

Chapter *1*

Due Process for Death: Jurek v. Texas and Companion Cases (1976)*

ON JULY 2 LAST, just two days less than two centuries since the United States of America sent its shining Declaration into the world, the Supreme Court declared itself on the matter of life and death.[1] After nearly ten years,

* Delivered as the Twelfth Annual Pope John XXIII Lecture on October 22, 1976, at the Catholic University of America.

I am grateful for research assistance, and helpful suggestions, to Seth Waxman, Yale Law School Class of 1977. Mr. Waxman, of course, has no responsibility for any of the views expressed.

1. Roberts v. Louisiana, 96 S. Ct. 3001 (1976); Woodson v. North Carolina, 96 S. Ct. 2978 (1976); Profitt v. Florida, 96 S. Ct. 2960 (1976); Jurek v. Texas, 96 S. Ct. 2950 (1976); Gregg v. Georgia, 96 S. Ct. 2909 (1976).

killing by law is to be resumed in the United States of America.

I oppose the penalty of death on many grounds, some rationally arguable and some not. Fully to argue those grounds which are arguable, and fairly to confess and to illustrate those sentiments which are not arguable, is not the work of this lecture. The Supreme Court has given us a much smaller subject to consider. Opinions in five cases, all decided on that same July 2, give us the reasons for the Court's holding that infliction of death may be resumed under the statutes approved. I shall here say something of what I think about the sufficiency and coherency of these reasons, not traveling outside the opinions themselves.

For background, we need go no further than Furman v. Georgia,[2] decided in 1972. I will compress an oft-told tale. Looking over the five opinions on the prevailing side in *Furman*, the fair view would have to be that the minimal ground, on which all five could probably agree, lay somewhere in the area of the mode of administration of the death penalty, and that this defect in administration lay in the arbitrariness, the lack of what I may clumsily call rule-boundedness, of the choice, amongst all eligible defendants, of those who were to die.

So the matter was seen, in any case, by some two-thirds of the state legislatures. New death-penalty statutes were widely enacted. These fell into two broad categories—the guide-to-discretion category and the mandatory-death category.

Five of these statutes came to the bar of the Court in its October 1975 Term, and these statutes, with the death sentences imposed under them, were the subjects of the five decisions of July 2, 1976. All three of the "rules for

2. 408 U.S. 238 (1972).

discretion" statutes were upheld.[3] Both of the "mandatory" statutes were struck down.[4]

The "rules for discretion" cases were from Georgia, Texas, and Florida. Let us ask, then, what sort of system for guiding jury choice between life and death has been held to satisfy the Constitution of the United States. For the answer, we must focus on Jurek v. Texas.[5] I say this because the Texas statute seems to me to be so much worse than either the Georgia or the Florida statutes, bad as these are, that it, and not they, sets the constitutional outpost, as that outpost can now be known. Throughout, I shall concentrate on the Texas case, relating it to the others.

The Georgia decision is first announced, and the plurality opinion (read by Mr. Justice Stewart, for himself and Justice Powell and Stevens) points with something almost like pride to what are seen as the "clear and objective standards"[6] of the Georgia statute, and especially to its provisions for appellate review of the death sentence, not only for "error" but for consistency with practice in other cases in the state, and even for absence of passion or prejudice.

Judgment is also announced in the Florida case. The plurality opinion here (delivered, for the same three Justices, by Mr. Justice Powell) stresses the similarity of the Florida to the Georgia statute in the particulars just mentioned.

In between these two statutes, which are at least

3. Profitt v. Florida, 96 S. Ct. 2960 (1976); Jurek v. Texas, 96 S. Ct. 2950 (1976); Gregg v. Georgia, 96 S. Ct. 2909 (1976).
4. Roberts v. Louisiana, 96 S. Ct. 3001 (1976); Woodson v. North Carolina, 96 S. Ct. 2978 (1976).
5. 96 S. Ct. 2950 (1976).
6. 96 S. Ct. at 2936, *citing with approval* Coley v. State, 231 Ga. 829, 834, 204 S.E.2d 612, 615 (1974).

elegantly structured, walks (or is supported as it stumbles) the Texas statute. Let us look at it very closely, and at the plurality opinion (by the same Justices) upholding it, for it, as I have said, states the now-known requirements of constitutional law, as opposed to mere beaming approval from the high bench. Georgia and Florida can tomorrow repeal all the features the Court so admires in their statutes, and copy the Texas statute verbatim, and still be within the law as the Court has declared it.

The Texas sentencing statute occurs in a technical context newly weird and wonderful to me every time I look at it. Let me bridge it over by starting with the sentencing procedure, once a killing has been found to fall within one of the "capital" categories. The Court thus describes this:

> In addition, Texas adopted a new capital-sentencing procedure. See Texas Code of Crim. Proc., Art. 37.071 (Supp. 1975–1976). That procedure requires the jury to answer three questions in a proceeding that takes place subsequent to the return of a verdict finding a person guilty of one of the above categories of murder. The questions the jury must answer are these:
> "(1) whether the conduct of the defendant that caused the death of the deceased was committed deliberately and with the reasonable expectation that the death of the deceased or another would result;
> "(2) whether there is a probability that the defendant would commit criminal acts of violence that would constitute a continuing threat to society; and
> "(3) if raised by the evidence, whether the conduct of the defendant in killing the deceased was unreasonable in response to the provocation, if any, by the deceased." Texas Code Crim. Proc., Art. 37.071(b) (Supp. 1975–1976).
> If the jury finds that the State has proved beyond a

reasonable doubt that the answer to each of the three questions is yes, then the death sentence is imposed.[7]

Now this list will puzzle any law student who has had an elementary course in criminal law, because he will recognize Question 1 as inquiring about the actual or constructive intent to kill, without an affirmative finding on which nobody would have been convicted of first degree murder at all, and in Question 3 he will recognize an inquiry which in most cases must already have been answered by the jury, if raised by the evidence, in finding first-degree murder rather than murder without malice or manslaughter. Inspection of the Texas statutes, with which I will not weary you, confirms these obvious points.[8]

The jury, therefore, is nearly always asked to make a "finding" on only one question not already answered. If, indeed, a jury answered "no" to either Question 1 or Question 3, I should think the conviction of first-degree murder, to which the sentencing procedure is a sequel, would in any civilized system of justice have to be set aside, on the ground that it was obviously reached through misapprehension.

The second question, then, is, at the very least, almost always going to be the only one on which the jury actually decides anything it has not already decided. It is the life-or-death question.

Remember that the jury must find "yes" beyond a reasonable doubt on this question before a death sentence may be imposed. Remember, too, that the defendant is

7. 96 S. Ct. at 2955.
8. Tex. Penal Code §§ 19.02, 19.04 (effective Jan. 1, 1974). The predecessor statutes, not for the present purpose materially different, are VERNON'S ANN. PENAL CODE §§ 1256, 1257b, 1257c (1961).

in any case going to the penitentiary for life, and can, beyond any doubt, reasonable or otherwise, be denied parole and kept indoors if the state's own agency thinks him a threat to society at large. Thus, in this context, the jury is being asked, "Is it true beyond a reasonable doubt that there is a probability that this defendant would commit criminal acts of violence that would constitute a continuing threat to society, while he is confined in the penitentiary, or years later, when he is released on parole—which need not happen if he has been seriously violent in the penitentiary or shown any threatening signs while there?"

I have said during this last year, before July 2, that I did not see how any lawyer could at any time have upheld such a statute as against a "due process" objection. I should have thought that Mr. Justice McReynolds would have struck it down in 1925. Why have I been saying this? Let me particularize—for that which has seemed to me so obvious must now be searchingly, even tediously, examined.

(1) The concept of the existence of a "probability" "beyond a reasonable doubt" is and can be only puzzling—even mind-boggling—to a jury or to anybody. In strict mathematical terms, and in dealing with a subject strictly amenable to mathematical treatment, it is of course possible to assert that there "is a probability" not only "beyond a reasonable doubt" but to a certainty. But non-mathematicians neither use language nor think in such a way. The terms "probability" and "beyond a reasonable doubt" are repugnant and at war with one another in the common speech in which juries, like all of us, talk and think.

(2) The word "probability" is itself triply ambiguous, and vague in at least two of its possible senses. In the

mathematical usage I have just cited, it means one thing—any chance, however small. There is, beyond any doubt, a probability that each of 100 successively tossed coins will come up heads—a probability, namely, of one in 2^{100}—and this has no necessary connection, by the way, with what will happen when you toss, for it is, to the mathematician, quite irrelevant that you may actually toss either far more or far less than 2^{100} sequences of 100 before all of one sequence are heads. All this may seem very technical. But if you think that in laymen's usage the word "probability" cannot sometimes mean "small probability," listen to the next weather forecast on television.

Quite another usage would define "probability" as "more than a 50 percent likelihood of occurrence." This may be a more widely diffused usage. But then, what does it mean to predicate, of a presently existing person, that it is beyond a reasonable doubt more than 50 percent likely that under radically altered circumstances he will do certain unlawful things? Does anybody think that you, or I, or a jury of twelve good persons and true, can otherwise than arbitrarily make that fine-grained a prediction? What technique of prediction is being referred to? Does anybody think that a jury understands the words this way unambiguously—or has any reason to?

Finally, though I doubt the commonness and even the correctness of this usage, "probability" may, and perhaps sometimes does, mean "high probability"— converging on a prediction "beyond a reasonable doubt" as a limit. If that is what is meant, then the term "probability" is wholly or partially short-circuited and the jury is asked to do something close—just how close we know not—to finding that the defendant will "beyond a reasonable doubt" do these things. But there are two things wrong with this. First, the jury is not told this. Second, there very surely exists no science of predicting human behavior which can reliably make such a prediction as to human beings "beyond a reasonable doubt." Any group of, say, nine mature persons ought to know that even if this question were asked clearly, as it is not, no jury really can predict "beyond a reasonable doubt" that X will cut up rough in the penitentiary.

(3) "Criminal acts of violence that would constitute a continuing threat to society" is a phrase composed of hopelessly vague terms. "Criminal" as a blow with the fist is criminal? "Violent" as such a blow is violent? A "threat" of what? "To society" in what sense, since the person is to be in prison, under whatever restraints the state finds necessary, and need not be released until the state is satisfied, to whatever degree it desires to be satisfied, that he is not a threat to society? If you think all this farfetched, then what do you do about the fact that this same plurality pointed with unequivocal approval, on this same July 2, to the fact that the Georgia court had held "impermissibly vague" the phrase "substantial history of serious assaultive criminal convictions?"[9]

I have been dissecting this statute with the aim, I suppose, of giving some scientific precision to its plain shabbiness, to its self-speaking insufficiency as law. A year ago, I would have thought that unnecessary. I would have thought that the trained intuition of any seasoned lawyer would recognize at once, in this grimly silly statute, something far beyond serious consideration—much as one can tell that a batter has struck out without cal-

9. 96 S. Ct. at 2939, *citing* Arnold v. State, 236 Ga. 534, 540, 224 S.E.2d 386, 391 (1976). This citation, in context, is by way (it seems) of removing what would else be a possible obstacle to the Georgia affirmance. How is it thinkable, then, that the problem in Texas Question 2 is not even worth mention, particularly since, in Jurek v. Texas, the "yes" answer to Question 2 was an indispensable step in the path to death, while the corresponding question was not directly raised in Gregg?

culating the number of nitrogen molecules between the
bat and the ball. But I do not think I have made a point
amiss; I think I have partly shown why, as ought to be
obvious without all this, a jury must either resolve all
these verbal puzzles for itself, without sufficient grounds
for the resolution chosen, or else proceed in puzzlement
to its own standardless decision—or do a bit of both.
What does the plurality opinion do with all this?
Well, nothing. The staggering fact is that this plurality
opinion, having clearly stated that defendant's counsel
had argued that Question 2 was "so vague as to be meaningless," then embarks upon and finishes a paragraph
which says nothing, absolutely nothing, about this
contention.[10] It vanishes from sight. Read if you doubt,
as well you may.

This is the way not of reason but of fiat—the fiat of
silence. I make bold to say that this way was chosen
because there is not and cannot be any satisfactory answer
as to the vagueness of this Texas statute. If it is to be
upheld, the difficulties about its vagueness must be ig-
nored, not discussed at all, and that is the path, I truly
regret having to say, that the plurality opinion in *Jurek*
selects. If reason, opened to public scrutiny, is the soul of
law, and if the decision for death is the most solemn decision law can make, then I am right in thinking that this
paragraph records one of the most disturbing and sorrowful moments in the long history of American constitutional judgment. Lest there be any question of inadvert-
ence, let me add that the vagueness problem, far from
being a mere off-spark of the fevered professorial brain,
was earnestly and most ably presented by the two judges
on the Texas Court of Criminal Appeals who dissented
from the affirmance of the death penalty in *Jurek* when

10. Jurek v. Texas, 96 S. Ct. 2950, 2957–58 (1976).

the case was in that court.[11] The Supreme Court plurality opinion does not even mention the existence of these dissents. They should, nevertheless, be read with care by anybody who thinks this vagueness question was insubstantial enough to be waved away without so much as a word of answer.

(Franz Kafka might have imagined, though here it is the solemn truth, that Mr. Justice White, in his concurring opinion, joined by the Chief Justice and Justice Rehnquist, says of the vagueness objection, "I agree with the plurality that the issues posed in the sentencing procedure have a common sense core of meaning and that criminal juries should be capable of understanding them."[12] The plurality opinion says nothing to which this *oratio obliqua* could refer. I feel some comment should be made about this, but I cannot devise any that seems condign.)

Having alluded separately to the defendant's vagueness contention and to his contention that "it is impossible to predict future behavior," the plurality opinion addresses itself only to the latter contention;[13] this is how the vagueness problem was made to get lost. The "prediction" contention is answered by pointing, with examples, to the fact that predictions of behavior are and must be made elsewhere in the criminal justice system. The examples chosen (and I hope we can assume that on a matter of this deadly seriousness they are not lightly chosen) are admission to bail, determination of the kind and duration of punishment other than death, and admission to parole. In pointing to these three areas, the plurality

11. Jurek v. State, 522 S.W.2d 934, 943, 946 (Tex. Crim. App. 1975) (Roberts, J., joined by Odom, J., dissenting).

12. 96 S. Ct. at 2955.

13. Id. at 2957–58.

opinion is pointing to three disaster areas in law as it stands. Who is satisfied with the law's performance in any of these fields? Does this performance justify the conclusion that prediction of future behavior "beyond a reasonable doubt"—not a requirement in any of these three areas—really is feasible? But deeper than that, what has happened now to the uniqueness of the death penalty? Has this eternal uniqueness somehow vanished since Mr. Justice Stewart spoke of it, as of a thing well known, in 1972?[14] Does the plurality really want to espouse the proposition that that which will do for admission or nonadmission to bail will do for death? If not, then is not the bail example merely diversionary, dust in the eyes?

What is wanted, and wanting, is an example, one single example in the whole range of civilized law outside of this one statute, that explicitly and in terms makes a person's cruel death depend on a prediction of that person's *future* conduct.

Now let me draw your minds into another thing about this judgment and opinion. The plurality opinions in the Florida and Georgia cases, between which this Texas case is supported, make much—very much—of the appellate review in those states.[15] That review, say the writers of the plurality opinions, is a review for statewide consistency over time in the use of the death penalty. It is a fact proudly paraded that the appeals

14. Furman v. Georgia, 408 U.S. 238 (1972):

The penalty of death differs from all other forms of criminal punishment, not in degree but in kind. It is unique in its total irrevocability. It is unique in its rejection of rehabilitation of the convict as a basic purpose of criminal justice. And it is unique, finally, in its absolute renunciation of all that is embodied in our concept of humanity.

Id. at 306 (Stewart, J., concurring).
15. Profitt v. Florida, 96 S. Ct. 2960, 2967 (1976); Gregg v. Georgia, 96 S. Ct. 2909, 2939–40 (1976).

courts in these two states may and do set aside death sentences as disproportionate, or as out of line with general practice.

When we get to Texas, the plurality opinion says:

> By providing prompt judicial review of the jury's decision in a court with statewide jurisdiction, Texas has provided a means to promote the evenhanded, rational, and consistent imposition of death sentences under law.[16]

It is paradoxical that one must sometimes hope that carelessness is present in a judicial utterance, but I do hope this sentence was careless. If it was, it was very careless. For there is no reason to think that the Court of Criminal Appeals in Texas reviews for anything like death sentence proportionality or consistency, or for anything other than "error," normally defined, in the very case. That which was so praised in the two other cases, to the point of its presence's seeming to be geared into the *ratio decidendi*, is apparently not necessary at all, not even as a grace-note, as a matter of constitutional law.

Another appalling thing about this Texas case cannot be understood unless we turn briefly to the Louisiana and North Carolina cases.[17] In these cases the Court struck down the two statutes at bar on the grounds:

(1) That mandatory death sentences for murder violate the eighth amendment, because society has evolved a judgment that death should be reserved for the worst offenders, as evidenced by the many statutes giving juries discretion in sentencing—the statutes invalidated in *Furman*.[18]

---

16. Jurek v. Texas, 96 S. Ct. 2950, 2958 (1976).
17. Roberts v. Louisiana, 96 S. Ct. 3001 (1976); Woodson v. North Carolina, 96 S. Ct. 2978 (1976).
18. 96 S. Ct. at 3006 (*Roberts*); 96 S. Ct. at 2983–90 (*Woodson*).

(2) Clearly as an independently sufficient ground, that the making mandatory of the death penalty would result in jury evasion, taking the form either of acquittal or of a verdict of "guilty" of a lesser offense, whatever the state of the evidence, which would be the functional equivalent of full discretion, condemned in *Furman*.[19]

The first of these grounds, it is important to note, stands up, in the Court's mind, whether or not the mandatorily capital offenses are narrowly defined, as in Louisiana.[20]

Now the Louisiana categories of capital murder are not altogether identical with the Texas categories, but these differences, I submit, cannot be of constitutional significance. Thus the Texas case stands as the extreme in not one but two series. On one view, it is the extreme to which states may constitutionally go in setting up, or perhaps I should say in not setting up, "standards" or "guides." In its second aspect, it stands as the limit in the "mandatory" line, for it materially differs from the condemned Louisiana statute only in its requirement of "yes" answers to the Texas questions, which I have just thoroughly discussed, as a prerequisite to a death sentence. Louisiana need only amend its statute so that it asks the three Texas questions, just as I have shown them to you, and its defect is cured.

Let me turn now to another facet of confrontation between the Texas case—as well as the Georgia and Florida cases—and the "mandatory" cases. In the Louisiana and North Carolina cases, the Court clearly says that a separate deficiency of the statute is that (in brief paraphrase) it encourages jury refusal to convict, or to convict of a lesser offense, whatever the evidence. The

19. 96 S. Ct. at 3007–08 (*Roberts*); 96 S. Ct. at 2990–91 (*Woodson*).
20. 96 S. Ct. at 3004–06.

point is made several times, but strikingly in the following sentences from the North Carolina case:

> It is argued that North Carolina has remedied the inad-
> equacies of the death penalty statutes held unconstitutional in
> *Furman* by withdrawing all sentencing discretion from juries
> in capital cases. But when one considers the long and con-
> sistent American experience with the death penalty in first-
> degree murder cases, it becomes evident that mandatory
> statutes enacted in response to *Furman* have simply papered
> over the problem of unguided and unchecked jury discre-
> tion. . . .

In view of the historic record, it is only reasonable to assume
that many juries under mandatory statutes will continue to
consider the grave consequences of a conviction in reaching a
verdict. North Carolina's mandatory death penalty statute provides no standards to guide the jury in its inevitable exercise of
the power to determine which first-degree murderers shall live
and which shall die. And there is no way under the North
Carolina law for the judiciary to check arbitrary and capricious
exercise of that power through a review of death sentences.
Instead of rationalizing the sentencing process, a mandatory
scheme may well exacerbate the problem identified in
Furman by resting the penalty determination on the particular
jury's willingness to act lawlessly.[21]

But these lawless juries, whose lawlessness will taint
and bend a mandatory system, are the very same juries
who are going to follow with patient care the intricacies
of the Georgia and Florida statutes, and the unfathomed
mysteries of the Texas statute, and base their answers on
nothing but sound discretion guided by law. Of course
the institution of the jury undergoes no such metamor-
phosis at a state line, or between one function and
another. If you cannot even trust a jury to follow the
evidence in finding what degree of murder has occurred,

21. 96 S. Ct. at 2990–91.

or indeed whether the accused is guilty at all, then it is cruelly preposterous to trust a jury to apply a law-guided and unperturbed "discretion" in that assessment and counterweighing of "aggravating" and "mitigating" circumstances required in Florida and Georgia. If "jury lawlessness" is a problem—and the history adduced by the plurality opinions in the Louisiana and North Carolina cases seem to establish this beyond doubt—then what do you expect of a jury that is trying to make out and apply the "law" of Question 2 in the Texas statute? Such a jury, perhaps, cannot be "lawless," for there is no law to follow, but it can be as wayward, as obedient to its own obscure impulses, as it wishes to be.

I move now to a pervading point in all these cases. I take you back to Mr. Justice Stewart's phrase in *Furman:* "a legal system."[22]

A principal contention of all the defendants in the July 2 decisions was that even if (as was not the case, in their view and mine) the Texas, Georgia, and Florida cases met the *Furman* standard as to the sentencing stage, the "legal systems" for administering the criminal law, in all American states, contain, at not one but at a number of crucial points, too much arbitrary discretion to make them suitable, or decently usable, for the processing of the question, "Who is to die?" This discretion exists as to the prosecutor, who decides, without constraints, what to charge, and who holds in his hands control over the enormously important decision whether the accused person is to be allowed to plead guilty to a lesser charge. It exists in the jury's virtually uncontrollable power to find "not guilty" or "guilty" of a lesser offense—a power the reality and importance of which was recognized and made a ground for decision even by the Supreme Court plurality that prevailed in the July 2 Louisiana and North Carolina cases. It exists in the decision on insanity—a decision for the making of which the law has notoriously failed to provide intelligible standards. It exists in the administration of clemency. The net effect of all this is that, quite aside from the step formally devoted to a sentencing decision, the actual selection of persons for death is made by a series of choices not governed by any articulated standards. It is not meant that persons exercising discretion at each of these stages behave lawlessly in any pejorative sense of that word. The point, rather, is that they are given—and perhaps can be given—no law to follow.

It would be ostentatiously and uncharacteristically self-effacing of me not to mention that I published a book a couple of years ago on this aspect of the administration of the death penalty.[23] The main reason, however, for my mentioning this book is that, as far as I have seen —and I read reviews as eagerly as the next author—no reviewer, whether approving or disapproving of the *conclusion* I reached, has even attempted to fault my *description* of the criminal justice system, as one simply saturated with uncontrolled discretion and proneness to error.

In all the cases decided on July 2, it was urged upon the Court that such a system was unsuitable for making the choice for the "unique and irreversible" penalty of death. I now urge upon you that the Court's answer to this contention was insufficient. This answer is scattered throughout the opinions, but is perhaps best summed up in the Georgia case's plurality opinion:

23. C. Black, *Capital Punishment: The Inevitability of Caprice and Mistake* (first ed., 1974).

The existence of these discretionary stages is not determinative of the issues before us. At each of these stages an actor in the criminal justice system makes a decision which may remove a defendant from consideration as a candidate for the death penalty. *Furman*, in contrast, dealt with the decision to impose the death sentence on a specific individual who had been convicted of a capital offense. Nothing in any of our cases suggests that the decision to afford an individual defendant mercy violates the Constitution. *Furman* held only that, in order to minimize the risk that the death penalty would be imposed on a capriciously selected group of offenders, the decision to impose it had to be guided by standards so that the sentencing authority would focus on the particularized circumstances of the crime and the defendant.[24]

This reply is defective. First of all, it makes the resolution of the problem hinge on whether prior decisions, especially *Furman*, compel the acceptance of the argument; that undoubtedly commends itself as the easier way out (though not, in my view, open even on its own merits), but it is a way out that is not even relevant to an argument which is—as this one was, and as so many successful constitutional arguments have been—genuinely new. The question is not whether *Furman*, or any other prior decision, *compels* the acceptance of this new argument, but whether it is convincing in itself.

I think, however, that the dismissal of *Furman*, as not speaking at all to the question, was wrong. I would be surprised if anyone were willing to espouse, in clear terms, the view that uncontrolled discretion in a jury, when it comes to selecting a death sentence, is wrong, while uncontrolled discretion at all the other strategically located stations on the way to the electric chair is right. That kind of constitutional law is formal and trivial, and protects nothing of substance.

24. 96 S. Ct. at 2937.

Moreover, in the passage I have cited the plurality twists the issue in a manner that might tempt one to suspect a desire to avoid it. For the question posed is not whether "the decision to afford an individual defendant mercy violates the Constitution." The question, very clearly raised by counsel, and very clearly put by my own book, is whether a "legal system," which regularly, and in great numbers, runs the death question through a gauntlet of decisions in no way even formally standard-bound, so that, at the end of the process, no one can say why some were selected and others were not selected for death, rises to due process. That is not a trivial question, and it cannot be answered by squeezing it down to a question about an individual defendant or by a caricature of its tenor.[25] Nor is it answered by calling it, as Mr. Justice White does, "in final analysis an indictment of our entire system of justice."[26] If it is that, it is an indictment pleading to which would present some difficulty, for it is hard to find informed persons today who think very well of our "entire system" of criminal justice. But death is unique, and the procedures we must use, having no better, in our entire system of justice—and that is really the kindest thing one can say of that system—may still not be good enough for the death choice. The Court has not really

25. The caricature (96 S. Ct. at 2937 n. 50) consists in the imagination of a sort of automatized movement of persons toward death. That would, indeed, be horrible. So is the papered-over arbitrariness now sanctioned by the Court. To show that one is horrible has no tendency, logical or pragmatic, to show that the other is not. Perhaps what is really brought to light here is the dilemma into which society is brought when it resolves on official killing. This dilemma may be—I think it is—quite insoluble. Whatever the answer to this wider question, the system we *now* have is as it is, and the Texas, Florida, and Georgia procedures are as they are, and they are not made any better by imagining horrible alternatives—which need not be adopted, because a much simpler solution is at hand.

26. 96 S. Ct. at 2949. Mr. Justice White goes on to say, "Mistakes will be made and discriminations will occur which will be difficult to explain." Yes.

focused on and answered that question—in reason, I mean, and not by fiat.

Now there is a great deal more to say about these decisions than can be said within the limits of one lecture. I think I have done right in focusing mainly on the Texas case, for it is the case that counts, as a matter of law and not as a matter of approved embellishment. But let me just make a few more rather sparely stated points, which you might want to check out in the opinions.

First, the Georgia and Florida sentencing statutes are not nearly as good as the Court makes them sound. In Georgia, underneath all the verbiage of the statute, the fact is that the jury, on no grounds or on any grounds, articulated or not articulated, can spare any defendant's life either by refusing to sentence to death though "aggravating circumstances" be found, or, as is more likely, simply failing, whatever the evidence, to find aggravating circumstances—both being unreviewable actions. The strictly logical corollary is that the jury may, within the same field of death eligibles, fail to spare some others, and need give no reason for the difference. Arbitrary lenience equals arbitrary harshness, by an iron law of sheer identity. This is not, after all, so different even from *Furman*—and I remind you that the plurality's reference to "jury lawlessness" as to a thing known, in the "mandatory" cases, brings this possibility within the high-probability range. The Florida situation, while differing technically, is not substantially different.

Secondly, the Florida case, on its facts and findings, is virtually a textbook illustration of the total malleability of these "circumstances" statutes. The worst factual case possible, on the evidence, was that the defendant had broken into the deceased's house, stabbed the deceased with a knife, hit the deceased's wife (the only other person present) with his fist, and fled. On this record, the trial judge supported his death sentence with four "findings" of statutory "aggravating circumstances," two of which were that "the murder was especially heinous, atrocious and cruel" and that "the petitioner knowingly, through his intentional act, created a great risk of serious bodily harm and death to *many* persons."[27] These "findings" stood up in the Florida appellate court, though, as to the first, that court had previously seemed to confine this "circumstance" to "the conscienceless or pitiless crime which is unnecessarily torturous to the victim." The Supreme Court plurality opinion tries to deal with all this by invoking the technicalities of "error."[28] But nothing can exorcise the facts: (1) that a typical stabbing, not shown to be any more than that, may be found (or of course *not* found) to be "especially heinous, atrocious or cruel," and (2) that *"many* persons" may in Florida mean *two* persons, one of whom was not even shown to be threatened with death or great bodily harm. Who could ask for a better illustration of the totally standardless discretion these new statutes afford?

Thirdly, the treatment of the deterrence question is plainly unsatisfactory. Correctly, and quite clearly, the plurality opinion in Gregg v. Georgia[29] notes that the question remains quite unsettled amongst the people competent to settle it. Then it proceeds to some pure conjecture of its own. Finally, it genuflects to federalism:

The value of capital punishment as a deterrent of crime is a complex factual issue the resolution of which properly rests

27. 96 S. Ct. at 2964 (emphasis added).
28. 96 S. Ct. at 2968 n.13. The assumption behind this footnote in the plurality opinion is that, since there was enough evidence of one aggravating circumstance at least, it didn't matter about the others. This is, charitably, a bizarre application of the concept of "weighing."
29. 96 S. Ct. 2909 (1976).

with the legislatures, which can evaluate the results of statistical studies in terms of their own local conditions and with a flexibility of approach that is not available to the courts.[30]

Now that is nothing but sheer fiction. How could it be possible, in fact and not in fiction, that state legislatures really possess some superior capability of resolving correctly, in application to their own populations, a question on which the most competent students utterly disagree? I intend nothing derogatory in this—I only attribute to the legislatures an ignorance which the Court, rightly, attributes to mankind, and to which I cheerfully confess in myself. The law, to be sure, is full of fictions, but a fiction known to go in the face of fact ought to play no part, not the slightest, in deciding whether the state may rightly take a life.

I am sure I weary you, without beginning to exhaust my subject. I want to close with a concreteness, taking you back to my native Texas. Down there a young man named Smith is awaiting execution. Smith was party to a filling-station robbery, in the course of which an attendant was killed. The uncontradicted evidence showed that Smith did not kill the attendant—a confederate did that. There was contradictory testimony as to whether Smith even attempted to; the evidence against him on this issue was an "oral confession" contradicting his trial testimony—with all the confidence such a confession inspires. He had once been convicted on a charge of possessing marijuana; that was his whole criminal record. A psychiatrist examined him for an hour and a half in all, administering a battery of tests, and testified to the opinion that Smith felt no remorse, that his conduct in the future would not change, and that he was a "sociopath." He was shown to have a poor employment record.

30. 96 S. Ct. at 2931.

The Texas Court of Criminal Appeals affirmed a death sentence[31] over scathing dissent. The dissent, uncontradicted by anything adduced elsewhere, pointed out that the psychiatrist's entire diagnosis and prognosis rested on one judgment alone, namely, that Smith, at the critical point in the testing, showed no "remorse." The majority said, in its brush-forward opinion: "Of extreme importance"—I repeat—"Of extreme importance is his apparent surrender to misfortune following his marijuana conviction." This on the issue of life or death!

Now in this case the jury answered "yes" to Question 1: "Whether the conduct of the defendant that caused the death of the deceased was committed deliberately and with the reasonable expectation that the death of the deceased or another would result," although no conduct of the defendant, in the strict sense, could be said to have caused death. It answered "yes" to Question 2—under "reasonable doubt" instructions, mind you—on the evidence I have summarized.

That is where we stand in Texas. Where does the Smith case stand in the Supreme Court? Well, it's not there yet, technically, but the plurality opinion in *Jurek*, in what to me is a stunningly prejudicial gesture, reaches out to embrace it, giving it as an illustration of the approved dealings of the Texas court and inferentially of Texas juries. In its brief summary, the plurality does not find time to mention that Smith had not killed anybody, though it does find time to speak of "his apparent wil-

31. Smith v. State, No. 49,809 (Tex. Crim. App. 1976). This opinion was withdrawn pending petition for rehearing but was reinstated and the dissents withdrawn, following the Supreme Court's July decisions. See Smith v. State, 540 S.W. 2d 693, 700 (Tex. Crim. App. 1976). All this of course, does not bear on the meaning of the Supreme Court's treatment of the case (described in the text, *infra*) which was as of the time of the citation first given here—but it does show how plainly the Supreme Court was taken to have decided the Smith case *before a certiorari petition had been so much as filed.*

lingness to kill" and "his lack of remorse after the killing." And one phrase occurs which has, to me, a haunt-
ing importance, symptomatic if not intrinsic. Referring
to what we know, if we read the Texas dissent, was a "five
year probated sentence for possessing marijuana," the
plurality opinion speaks (and listen to this) of "his prior
conviction on narcotics charges."[32]

I would have thought—and evidently I have much
to learn—that we live in a world where evidence of prior
conviction for the possession of marijuana would be simply excluded, as totally lacking probative value on the
Question 2 issue, and as potentially prejudicial. That is
the world inhabited in desire, I am proud to say, by my
two dissenting fellow-Texans down in Austin. In their
world, as in mine, failure to seek employment—*failure to
seek employment*—would be excluded on the same
grounds, with, I should think, a rebuke to the prosecutor
who dared adduce it.

But we really live in another world. We live in a
world where, in our highest Court, the most trivial of all
possible drug offenses, one rather plainly on its way to
decriminalization, is hidden behind the imposing
phrase, of sinister suggestion, "prior conviction on narcotics charges." I have essayed some examination of some
of the reasonings of the July 2 opinions; if I had in brief to
illustrate their tone I would point to this transformation.

I invite you to consider whether statutes which need
such reasonings and such tonalities to uphold them are
not in truth—in that truth no Court can alter-
—conspicuous illustrations of the fact that our legal system, after years of travail since *Furman*, cannot produce
a procedure fit for choosing people to die. If you go on

32. 96 S. Ct. at 2957.

from that to a still wider judgment on the capacity of man's justice, I welcome you.

For many reasons of respect and affection, I accepted the invitation to give this lecture at a time when I was really too busy. But the reason that most swayed my heart was that the series bears the name that is to me the most sanctified name of the century into which I was born. I know I have spoken with anger; in this case, I would be ashamed not to be and steadfastly to remain angry. But I hope and wish that I may have said nothing unworthy of a series bearing that name.

Chapter 2

The Death Penalty
Now (1977)*

IT WAS BRANDEIS, I believe, who said that no question is
ever settled until it is settled right. To the committed
combatant, the right settlement of a question cannot be
other than the settlement perceived by himself as right, as
it is given him to see the right. To me and to many
others, the capital-punishment question will not be settled until people are no longer put to death by law.

I am very sure that this question cannot be laid to
rest by such reasoning as was brought forward by the
Supreme Court on last July 2, in support of its judgments affirming death sentences in Georgia, Florida, and

* Delivered as the 1977 George Abel Dreyfous Lecture at Tulane University,
with minor textual changes. Thanks are due to Seth Waxman, Yale Law School '77,
for valuable research help and ideas, though he is of course in no way responsible for
the views expressed herein.

Texas.[1] I have elsewhere examined that reasoning,[2] and will not here do so again. Sometimes, in a long continuing struggle, one has to draw this kind of draft on one's previous work; only by presentation at the bank can it be determined whether the draft will be honored, and I invite you to read my Pope John XXIII lecture, to go from it to the July 2 opinions it examines, and to judge for yourself whether I was right in seeing in that July 2 "one of the most troubling and sorrowful moments in the long history of American constitutional judgment."[3]

With you on this occasion, in a lecture meant to be self-contained, I am going to start motion outward from these July 2 cases, into some of their wider implications, and sketch the position as I see it today.

Let us consider Sandra Lockett, who is now on death row in Ohio. Her conviction "in connection" with a homicide has been affirmed in the highest court of the state.[4] I stress the phrase "in connection," the phrase used by the Ohio Supreme Court in stating the case, because, in the ordinary usage of words, Sandra Lockett did not kill anybody, did not try to kill anybody, did not suggest that anybody be killed, and did not know anybody would be killed. Indeed, on the not faintly contradicted testimony of the state's principal witness at her trial, nobody at all intended or anticipated that anyone would be killed on the occasion in question.[5] How then did Sandra Lockett, in a nation wherein a murder occurs

1. Proffitt v. Florida, 96 S. Ct. 2960 (1976); Jurek v. Texas, 96 S. Ct. 2950 (1976); Gregg v. Georgia, 96 S. Ct. 2909 (1976).
2. In my Pope John XXIII Lecture at Catholic University, Black, *Due Process for Death: Jurek v. Texas and Companion Cases*, 26 Cath. U.L. Rev. 1 (1977) [hereinafter cited as Black].
3. Id. at p. 113 in this book.
4. State v. Lockett, 358 N.E.2d 1062 (Ohio 1976).
5. Id. at 1067, 1070.

every twenty-six minutes,[6] find herself among the three
hundred or so people on death row?

On January 15, 1975, Sidney Cohen was shot and
killed in his pawnshop in Akron. Sandra Lockett and
three other people were arrested. One of these, Parker,
accepted a negotiated plea, thus saving his own life,
though he was the actual gunman, in return for his coop-
eration with the state. His testimony[7] was substantially all
the evidence against Sandra Lockett; there was some general corroboration on the fringes, but no case could have
gotten to the jury without Parker's testimony; it stands,
without significant addition, as the whole case.

Skipping details, Parker's story was that Sandra
Lockett suggested a robbery as a means of getting some
needed money, and led the group to the pawnshop.
There was at no time any talk of killing anybody. Sandra
Lockett stayed outside in the car. During the hold-up,
the victim grabbed for the gun (held by Parker), which
then accidentally went off. Parker and his companions
fled. Parker rejoined Sandra Lockett in the car, and she
and he drove away. No other testimony contradicted or
tended to contradict this story.

Aggravated murder, of which Sandra Lockett was
convicted, is defined in the Ohio code as follows:

§ 2903.01.   Aggravated Murder

(a) No person shall purposely, and with prior calculation
and design, cause the death of another.

(b) No person shall purposely cause the death of another
while committing or attempting to commit, or while fleeing
immediately after committing or attempting to commit kidnapping, rape, aggravated arson or arson, aggravated robbery
or robbery, aggravated burglary or burglary, or escape.

6. N.Y. *Times*, March 20, 1977, at E3, col. 2.
7. 358 N.E.2d at 1070.

(c) Whoever violates this section is guilty of aggravated murder, and shall be punished as provided in section 2929.02 of the Revised Code.[8]

Since on the testimony of the state's own principal witness, uncontradicted by anything else, nobody purposely killed anybody in this case, and Sandra Lockett was absent from the scene, how did Sandra Lockett qualify for conviction of this offense? The answer, of course, lies in a process of "constructions." The use of a deadly weapon "constructively" establishes an intent to kill on Parker's part, though he, the state's one crucial witness, denied having such an intent in fact, no other evidence suggested he had it, and the "accident" story is not inherently implausible. Sandra Lockett's participation in the "conspiracy" makes her a "constructive" participant in Parker's "constructive" intent, though there is not even any serious contention, not so much as a conjecture, that she had such an intent. The paragraph concluding this series of "constructions" is worth quoting:

Therefore, the appellant, as well as the other participants is bound by all the consequences naturally and probably arising from the furtherance of the conspiracy to commit the robbery. The record reflects that this was the case and establishes beyond a reasonable doubt that the appellant had a purposeful intent to kill.[9]

Here we see a forced turn back into the world of assertions that sound as though they were assertions about psychological fact. But we must remember that this is a mere *tour de force*—or, perhaps better, a *trompe d'oeil*. No matter what fictions are set up, no matter what is equated with what in contemplation of law, the undis-

8. Ohio Rev. Code Ann. §2903.01 (Baldwin 1975).
9. 358 N.E.2d at 1072.

puted facts are that Sandra Lockett killed no one, and had no knowledge or intention that anyone would be killed.

Now at this point I face one of the greatest difficulties, I think, faced by those of us who are fighting against the penalty of death. It is rare that the condemned person can be shown not to have done anything very wrong. Sandra Lockett cannot be cleared of having committed a very serious offense, for which she must of course be punished by long imprisonment. But her serious culpability is not intended to be brought into question. What is in question is the rightness of her suffering death. When someone seeks to convert the question whether someone should die into the question whether that person has done any wrong, there may be momentary embarrassment for the opponent of the death penalty. But it is the proponent who should be embarrassed; for it is plainly he who is trying to cloud and evade the only question under discussion.

I submit that most temperate and emotionally controlled people who favor capital punishment have in mind, as the archetypal case, what is known as the "cold-blooded killer." The section of the Code under which Sandra Lockett was convicted read as though it applied to the cold-blooded killer, or at least to the killer who meant to kill.[10] What layman reading it, and making up his mind on it, or writing his legislative representative in support of it, would dream it referred to the case of a woman sitting in the car while somebody else, one of her confederates, accidentally killed a robbery victim?

It is by no means unimportant that the Sandra Lockett case was decided in the Ohio court by a 4–3

10. The statute provides, in relevant part: "No person shall *purposely cause* the death of another while committing . . . aggravated robbery. . . ." Ohio Rev. Code Ann. § 2903.01(B) (Baldwin 1975) [emphasis added].

margin, with a vigorous dissent. This dissent is on the very point I have been discussing; it rejects the mere "constructive" imputation to Sandra Lockett of an intent to kill. It proceeds on grounds which sound to me at least as maintainable technically as are those of the majority. This is expectable. When law is straightforward in its references, there is not much room for difference of opinion. When a result ensues not from straightforward reference but from management of wholly manipulable fictions, nothing constrains even the most competent and honest professional mind to any one result.

Now you may still think Sandra Lockett should die. But if you do you must give up any thought—and this thought has played a great and perhaps critical part in the pro-execution literature—that only the worst, the most malignant and abandoned of deliberate killers, should die. More to the point, perhaps, if you have up to now fooled yourself into thinking that the new capital punishment statutes, enacted since the Furman[11] case, actually are succeeding, or are built to succeed, in selecting for death only the most vicious killers, ponder the case of Sandra Lockett, who killed no one, tried to kill no one, and neither knew nor intended that anyone was to be killed. If a reader of these words is by chance one of those many who, in public and in private, have addressed to me the question whether after all, it wasn't just plain good sense to kill the most vicious of deliberate killers, I now direct to that person, for reflection, the question, "What do you think in regard to Sandra Lockett?"

These are the bare bones of the Sandra Lockett case. But that case spins off many problems. Let us consider first the problem of Parker's testimony, the only evidence

11. Furman v. Georgia, 408 U.S. 238 (1972).

of weight against Sandra Lockett. Bear in mind that that testimony not only linked her physically with the crime, not only established her general assent to it, but made her the suggester of it, even to the point of her suggesting a pawnshop as the target. It is quite unwarranted to think that these details can have had no effect on the jury. Parker, as the Ohio court puts it, was the "triggerman."[12] The blame of Cohen's death was principally his. If anyone was to go to the chair, Parker would go. His trial was scheduled first. Before it opened, he entered a negotiated plea carrying a life sentence and turned state's evidence; there could of course be no serious pretense that these two events were unconnected. In another case arising out of the same facts,[13] the Ohio court reversed because a tape made by Parker, seriously contradicting his trial testimony, had not been allowed in evidence; I mention this in passing, lest it be assumed that everything Parker said was uncontestedly true.

I do not assert that Parker's testimony, on the fine points of Sandra Lockett's participation, was false; of course I do not know whether it was or not. Nor do I mean so much as to suggest that in this particular case the prosecutor did anything wrong, on the case as it came to his view. What I do say is this: Sooner or later we in America will have to face the problem of people's being convicted on the testimony of those who cooperate with the prosecution in return for a better deal on sentencing. If a prosecutor paid a man ten dollars out of petty cash to turn state's evidence, we would remove, disbar, and possibly imprison that prosecutor, and the conviction had on such evidence would be unhesitatingly reversed. Yet, for so great is what Jellinek called "the normative power of

12. 358 N.E.2d at 1070.
13. State v. Lockett, 358 N.E.2d 1077 (Ohio 1976).

the actual," we unreflectingly accept the fact that much
testimony that convicts people of crime is had in return
for a leniency above the range of reckoning in money.
But, you may say, that is the only way we can run
the criminal justice system. And I don't know that you
are wrong. Maybe you are right; many practices less than
ideal must, it seems, be accepted in our system of justice.
But if you are right, then I think another telling argument
against capital punishment rises into view. The possible
state's witness's crazed fear of the electric chair is too potent a weapon to put in the prosecutor's hand; it is distant
by an order-of-magnitude jump from the weapon of
longer as against shorter imprisonment. We may have to
use grossly interested testimony, given in return for less-
ening the terrible burden of punishment by incarcera-
tion. But I submit that we ought not to acquiesce in a
system that convicts people on testimony given in return
for relief from the fear of a grisly death. As a mere obvious corollary, a fortiori, no one should be put to death on
the basis of such testimony.

(In this very case, potential jurors were asked, on
qualification, whether they would be "troubled" by the
fact that the triggerman was saving his life by testifying,
and this qualifying question was specifically linked to
credibility.[14] The jurors were thus asked to disregard the
most gross and obvious fact affecting credibility of a witness.)

Let me turn from this to a closely connected aspect
of the case of Sandra Lockett—her own refusal of a
negotiated plea. The Ohio court's syllabus tells the story:

Appellant, approximately two weeks prior to trial, was
offered the negotiated plea of voluntary manslaughter and

14. Transcript, vol. 1, at 34–35, State v. Lockett, 358 N.E.2d 1062 (Ohio 1976).

aggravated robbery if she would cooperate with the state. This plea was rejected.

Prior to commencement of trial, on March 28, 1975, after the state had prepared its case, appellant was offered the negotiated plea of aggravated murder. This, too, was rejected. The offer was renewed on April 1, 1975, the date of trial, and was again rejected by appellant. On April 3, 1975, appellant was subsequently found guilty by a jury, of aggravated murder, with two specifications, and of aggravated robbery. The trial court, upon completion of the statutory requirements, found no mitigating circumstances and sentenced appellant to death, and the Court of Appeals affirmed.[15]

Again, there is the normative power of the actual; we are used to this sort of thing. But let us dash a little cold water on our faces and ask freshly, "Can we really stomach this?" To all practical intents and purposes, this woman is going to be killed because she insisted on being tried. Again, it may be inevitable that people who insist on being tried be punished more severely than those who do not. I am inclined to think plea-bargaining cannot and perhaps even should not be eradicated. But is not death too great a punishment for refusal to enter into this process? Is the state's interest in avoiding trial—which is basically an interest in economy—great enough that we can be willing to execute people for not serving it? Are you willing to acquiesce in a system that offers people a sporting chance, with the odds getting less favorable as trial approaches, to avoid electrocution by agreeing to go to prison?

Now you may say that, after all, this woman knew she was guilty, and ought to have pled. I find death by electric shock a pretty stiff penalty even for such recalcitrance. But in truth the case is a perfect one for illustrating the fallacy of this whole line of argument. She knew she

15. 358 N.E.2d at 1066.

was guilty—of what? Two out of three psychiatrists who examined her put her intelligence below dead average, and one of these put her "in the range of borderline mental retardation."[16] The third doctor rated her intelligence as "slightly above average."[17] She was hooked on methadone at least;[18] whether she was in withdrawal when these decisions on pleading were made does not appear. Could she have gotten into the Tulane Law School? Yet I think that is where she would have to be even to start trying to understand the theories on which she was held guilty of killing. My trembling guess is that she may have thought something like, "Killing? Why, I was in the car." If that was what she was thinking, three of the seven judges on Ohio's highest court thought she was right, and was therefore *not* guilty on *either* of the pleas offered her—though they put their views in somewhat more artful terms.[19] Are you really willing to keep running a system that electrocutes a woman like this because, with whatever feeble intellection, she made a guess as to her own guilt that was the same as the holding of three out of seven of Ohio's top judges? Or have you just supported capital punishment because you didn't at all know how it was working? Think a bit more, along these lines, about Sandra Lockett.

Turn this plea-bargaining business around. Assuming it is here to stay—and I do so assume—is not death too potent a weapon, in this context as in another one discussed above, to place in the hands of the prosecutor, as he fixes the terms to be offered, and suggests the wisdom of their acceptance? Is it not the message of this very

16. Ibid. at 1074.
17. Ibid.
18. Ibid. at 1066. She was taking it as "her heroin substitute." Ibid.
19. Id. at 1075 (Stern, J., dissenting).

case that you'd better not insist on your rights as you see or dimly feel them, better not rely on such a technicality as possible innocence of the charge you are asked to plead to, because four out of seven judges up there may bewilderingly do something like concluding that you had "beyond a reasonable doubt . . . a purposeful intent to kill,"[20] even though you know that, in every colloquial sense of these words, this is preposterous?

Let me for a moment move from Sandra Lockett's very case to consider the Ohio sentencing scheme, under which she was given the chair. I have already quoted to you the section on aggravated murder,[21] conviction of which is a prerequisite to further processing toward death. The next stage in that processing is the determination by the jury of the existence, beyond a reasonable doubt, of one or more of the "specifications" listed in the Ohio Code as the essential foundation for a sentence of death.[22] Of the seven statutory specifications, only two had any possible relevance to Sandra Lockett's case, and I assume that it was these that the jury found to exist:

§ 2929.04. **Criteria for Imposing Death or Imprisonment for a Capital Offense**
(a) Imposition of the death penalty for aggravated murder is precluded, unless one or more of the following is specified in the indictment pursuant to section 2941.14 of the Revised Code, and is proved beyond a reasonable doubt:

. . . .

(3) The offense was committed for the purpose of escaping detection, apprehension, trial, or punishment for another offense committed by the offender.

. . . .

(7) The offense was committed while the offender was

20. Id. at 1072.
21. See text at note 8 *supra*.
22. Ohio Rev. Code Ann. §2929.04(A) (Baldwin 1975).

committing, attempting to commit, or fleeing immediately
after committing or attempting to commit kidnapping, rape,
aggravated arson, aggravated robbery, or aggravated burglary.[23]

Putting aside for a moment the first of these, a curi-
ous thing appears as to the second. There is a very wide
overlap between this language and the language in the
definition, which I have quoted above, of "aggravated
murder." The only difference is that the nonaggravated
degrees of robbery, burglary, and arson, as well as the
aggravated degrees thereof, enter into the definition of
aggravated murder. But this difference would rarely have
effect, for the aggravated degrees of all three of these offenses involve danger to persons,[24] so that it is the aggravated degrees that would normally be present when death
occurs. In most cases, therefore, the jury considering
whether to find in the affirmative on this "specification"
would be deciding the same question it had already
decided in finding the defendant guilty of aggravated
murder of the "felony murder" type described in
§2903.01(B).

Yet—and here I am fascinated, for it is always fas-
cinating to see where the joker of unchecked discretion is
hidden in these statutes—there are two vital leeways
allowed. First, no prosecutor is compelled to put any
"specification" in the indictment; thus, in all practical
effect, the prosecutor has entire discretion to ask or not to
ask for, to make possible or impossible, the imposition of
a sentence of death.[25] Secondly, as to murder, rape, and
arson, no jury can really be accused of inconsistency if it
makes the offense an element in a conviction of aggra-

23. Id. §§2929.04(A)(3), (7).
24. Id. §§2909.02(A), 2911.01(A), .11(A).
25. See id. §2929.03(A).

vated murder but finds in the negative on the associated "specification," for it can always be said that the "aggravated murder" conviction rested on a jury finding, hidden in the general finding of "guilty," that the killing occurred in the course of simple robbery, burglary, or arson, rather than in the course of an aggravated degree of one of these. There is no way to force a jury to find the aggravation element to have been proved "beyond a reasonable doubt."

The cases of kidnapping and rape are handled differently. There are no "aggravated degrees" of these; a jury that found a defendant guilty of aggravated murder, on evidence showing that the killing occurred in connection with kidnapping or rape, and then found in the negative on specification (7), would be in a flatly inconsistent position, though it is not clear what could be done about it. One might at this point begin to think these sentences are "mandatory," and hence possibly within the ban of the Louisiana and North Carolina cases decided last July 2.[26] There is in Ohio, to be sure, allowance for some enumerated mitigating circumstances,[27] but not, one would think, for that full range of mitigating circumstances the Supreme Court seems to think requisite in a valid statute. This "mandatory" quality, however, is of marginal im-

26. Roberts v. Louisiana, 96 S. Ct. 3001 (1976); Woodson v. North Carolina, 96 S. Ct. 2978 (1976).

27. Ohio Rev. Code Ann. § 2929.04(B) (Page 1975) lists three mitigating circumstances:

(1) The victim of the offense induced or facilitated it.

(2) It is unlikely that the offense would have been committed, but for the fact that the offender was under duress, coercion, or strong provocation.

(3) The offense was primarily the product of the offender's psychosis or mental deficiency, though such condition is insufficient to establish the defense of insanity.

The burden of proof, by a "preponderance of the evidence," is upon the defendant. 358 N.E. 2d at 1074.

portance, for any Ohio jury, in any kidnapping plus killing or rape plus killing case, could find the killing to amount to "involuntary manslaughter,"[28] a felony of the first degree. The difference between aggravated murder and involuntary manslaughter, in these circumstances, would under Ohio law be the difference between "purposely causing" and merely "causing" the death; on such an issue of internal mental state, it would usually be impossible even in theory—and always impossible in procedure and practice—to fault a jury's finding of the lesser included offense. Instruction on that offense would have to be given in virtually every case.

The pattern of the Ohio law of homicide, under which Sandra Lockett has been sent to death row, is then a familiar one. There is at the least a nearly full spectrum of options open to prosecutor and jury and court as to punishment, regardless of what "really happened." I mark the words "really happened," because of course we never know, especially on crucial questions of mental state, what the facts were. There is not and obviously cannot be any independent proceeding to determine whether a prosecutor or a jury went wrong.

In the Sandra Lockett case, for example, the prosecutor might easily, in perfect good faith, have determined—in view of Parker's anticipated testimony, for the state, that the killing was accidental, and in view of the plain lack of any killing purpose on Sandra Lockett's part—that "involuntary manslaughter" was the proper charge. This thought is not the imagination of a lawyer who knows Ohio only from waiting in its larger railroad stations, but is exactly the conclusion of the three dissenting Ohio judges on the last state appeal.[29] Is it

28. Ohio Rev. Code Ann. §2903.04(A) (Baldwin 1975).
29. 358 N.E.2d at 1075–76 (Stern, J., dissenting).

fanciful to think a prosecutor might have come to the same conclusion they did?

Now all these options are of course known in full detail to all prosecutors. It is neither necessary nor fair to think that they manipulate them improperly; it is sufficient to point out that they necessarily choose without rule or standard. In the vast majority of cases, probably in all, no prosecutor has to go for the death penalty if, on all the facts and circumstances known to him, that penalty is in his view disproportionate. At the charging stage, and at the plea-bargaining stage, he has a full range of alternatives, involving what he considers to be suitably severe punishment less than death.

Virtually as complete a range of alternatives is available to the properly instructed jury. Does the jury know this? Perhaps a jury, deciding on guilt or innocence of lesser offenses, may not know the exact consequences, in the hard counted-out coin of punishment, of its actions. But as to death we have in Ohio the comfort of seeing common sense supported by the emphatic statement of the best local authority, the Supreme Court of Ohio, in State v. Bayless:

With regard to the former point, we cannot agree that it is preferable or even possible that the jury be prevented from knowing that their verdict might result in the defendant's execution. Certainly many potential jurors are aware that Ohio has reinstituted the death penalty for aggravated murder, and some may well be familiar with the system of aggravating specifications which permits imposition of the death penalty. Public awareness will also increase as more trials follow this new system. It is highly unlikely that a jury panel in a case of aggravated murder with specifications could be chosen, none of whose members know that capital punishment might result from the verdict. Impanelling jurors in reliance on any such unrealistic assumption is so likely to result in juries with

150

CAPITAL PUNISHMENT

members who cannot render an impartial finding that it approaches, if it does not reach, absolute certainty.[30]

This view was cited with approval in Sandra Lockett's case. Of course it is right, in Ohio and everywhere.

Even more august authority is invocable. In the two "mandatory death" cases decided last July 2, the Supreme Court struck down the Louisiana and North Carolina statutes.[31] A clearly stated independent ground for this result was that a mandatory death statute, coupled with unreviewable jury power to find not guilty or, usually, guilty of a lesser included offense, would result in juries in effect having and using the total discretion held impermissible in the Furman case. The critical passage is worth quoting here:

It is argued that North Carolina has remedied the inadequacies of the death penalty statutes held unconstitutional in *Furman* by withdrawing all sentencing discretion from juries in capital cases. But when one considers the long and consistent American experience with the death penalty in first-degree murder cases, it becomes evident that mandatory statutes enacted in response to *Furman* have simply papered over the problem of unguided and unchecked jury discretion. . . . In view of the historic record, it is only reasonable to assume that many juries under mandatory statutes will continue to consider the grave consequences of a conviction in reaching a verdict. North Carolina's mandatory death-penalty statute provides no standards to guide the jury in its inevitable exercise of the power to determine which first-degree murderers shall live and which shall die. And there is no way under the North Carolina law for the judiciary to check arbitrary and capricious exercise of that power through a review of death sentences. Instead of rationalizing the sentencing process, a

30. 357 N.E.2d 1035, 1047 (Ohio 1976).
31. Roberts v. Louisiana, 96 S. Ct. 3001 (1976); Woodson v. North Carolina, 96 S. Ct. 2978 (1976).

mandatory scheme may well exacerbate the problem identified in *Furman* by resting the penalty determination on the particular jury's willingness to act lawlessly.[32]

Now one cannot in decorum even ask the Supreme Court a question, let alone compel an answer. But I long to ask the subscribers to the just-quoted language why in the world, in the possible world, they think juries will manipulate frankly mandatory statutes, in order to produce a result seen as equitable, but will not manipulate, to the same ends, a scheme relatively sophisticated—but far from being beyond easy comprehension by people fitted to be on juries at all—such as the scheme in Ohio, or Texas, or Georgia, or Florida, or many other states. Is something known about Ohio juries that makes this impossible or even unlikely? Why can they not be expected, in the quoted euphemism, to "take into account the grave consequences" of an affirmative finding on one of Ohio's "specifications," or of a finding of "guilty" on a greater rather than a lesser charge? And if there is no reason for not expecting this, then how is Ohio's system, in this absolutely vital characteristic, different from the "mandatory" systems that were adopted in Louisiana and North Carolina, and struck down on last July 2? And if those Louisiana and North Carolina mandatory systems were too close for constitutional comfort to the discretionary system struck down in *Furman*,[33] why is not Ohio's system too close?

Now I never seem to get very far from Texas, for to touch my *solum natale* even in words causes me to rise refreshed—and surely nothing can more reinvigorate an opponent of the death penalty than recurrence to the Texas scene. Now, however, I want, for a reason which

32. Woodson v. North Carolina, 96 S. Ct. 2978, 2990–91 (1976).
33. Furman v. Georgia, 408 U.S. 238 (1972).

will appear, to present an account of a quite recent Texas case that had a most merciful outcome. The case is not reported officially, and I take my data from the *New York Times*.[34]

In a small Texas town, a man was worried about his son. The boy, twenty years old, was taking valium (a minor tranquilizer), smoking marijuana, drinking cheap wine, not working. He had not only ceased participating in sports but had actually been expelled from high school for wearing his hair too long. All this the father endured as best he could, but at last it came clear to him that no improvement was to be looked for. So he went into his son's room while his son was asleep, folded the boy's arms across his chest, and killed him with one shot in the temple.

In the subsequent judicial proceeding seemingly required by decorum, the jury deadlocked 9–3 for acquittal. The father then was allowed to plead guilty to voluntary manslaughter, and received a five-year probated sentence.

(I know you don't believe this. Go look it up in the *New York Times*.)

Now I've told you this story as a sort of background to a point about Ohio, Texas, and many other states—all the states, in fact, which spell out, in something corresponding to the Ohio "specifications," those kinds of killing which are to make the defendant eligible for death. The point—which may or may not be convertible into a constitutional argument, but which ought surely to be of the most anxious public concern—is that the selection of categories for capital murder seem to have little

34. *N.Y. Times*, Jan. 18, 1977, at 20, col. 4.

more than a random relation to any imaginable ranking of wickedness by normal people.

Accordingly to the *New York Times*, the father in Texas said, "Yes, I did it for him." I know of no reason for not believing him. But let us imagine a hypothetical case in which a father did the same thing because he was irresistibly interested in his son's girlfriend, or bitterly envied the boy's scholastic achievements, or had quarreled with him about his choice of a profession, or just unreasoningly hated him. And let us suppose that he did not shoot him—for the mere act of shooting may in itself import in some minds an impression of forthrightness and manliness—but poisoned him slowly, hoping to escape detection.

The thing I want to ask you to think about is that a father who slowly poisoned his son in hope of getting someplace with the son's girlfriend could not, by any stretch of the law's language, have received a death sentence in Texas. The act would not arguably fall within any of the Texas categories of capital murder.[35]

Do Texans really think it is less wicked to poison one's son for sexual motives, or through unreasoning hate, than it is to kill somebody in panic, accidentally, in the course of a burglary? I mean by this question, of course, to suggest something more general. I suggest that in no state do the "aggravating" and "mitigating" circumstances, or the "specifications," detailed in the statutes, begin to cover the moral ground which any sane citizen of that state would on reflection regard as entailing at least as much depravity as a killing in one of the specified categories.

35. See Tex. Penal Code Ann. tit. 5, § 19.03 (Vernon 1974).

Is Texas peculiar on this? Well, back to Ohio. Ohio has a longer list of specifications than does Texas. You could get the chair there for killing a candidate for lieutenant-governor, a "candidate" being defined as one who "has been nominated . . . according to law, or . . . has filed a petition [for nomination] . . . according to law, . . . or . . . [is] . . . a write-in candidate in a primary. . . ."[36] But you could not get the chair for poisoning your son for personal reasons. You could not, I think, get the chair if you poisoned him to collect on his insurance, because while the Texas specification of killing "for remuneration"[37] might conceivably stretch to fit, the Ohio phrase, "for hire,"[38] could not.

Now what I assert is that none of these state lists of particular circumstances qualifying the defendant for death is, on a full view of possibility, anything but an arbitrary selection. Particular instances cannot prove this. Instead, prove it for yourself. Take any one of these lists—the Ohio one would do—and make your own list of murders that are not covered, but that must be, to any reasonably normal citizen of Ohio or of any other state, just as bad as or worse than anything on the list. If you work at this a short while, your list will be longer than the one in the statute-books.

Or take, one last time, Sandra Lockett—who killed no one, tried to kill no one, intended no killing, and did not know that any killing was to take place. Sandra Lockett did a very wrong thing; within our presuppositions, she must be punished. But is a system tolerable, is a system close to tolerable, which will electrocute her and send to prison for life a man who clubs his wife to death

36. Ohio Rev. Code Ann. § 2929.04(A)(1) (Baldwin 1975).
37. Tex. Penal Code Ann. tit. 5, § 19.03(a)(3) (Vernon 1975).
38. Ohio Rev. Code Ann. § 2929.04(A)(2) (Baldwin 1975).

for her money, or through lust to live with another woman, and seeks to put the crime on somebody else? Would an Ohioan, perhaps, not call that discrimination "freakish and wanton"?[39]

There is no solution; the situation is dilemmatic, hopelessly so. To make all first-degree murder mandatorily punishable by death is, the Supreme Court has said, both a cruel and unusual punishment and an undeclinable invitation to jury lawlessness.[40] Coming from a court minded as that one was on that July 2, we can take this as right—though I have the irreverence to be even more impressed by its obvious rightness *in pais*. To give juries full discretion is settled as wrong under *Furman*.[41] The statutes put in place, like the Ohio statute I have examined today, and the Texas, Georgia, and Florida statutes I examined in my Pope John lecture,[42] paper over the problem, but do not, in result, furnish guides that can be understood and applied, or that can be warranted to be applied within the legal system as it stands, or that express any conceivable set of real moral judgments.

We did not create life; perhaps it is only a symmetry, whose final secret is hidden from us, that decrees that whichever way we turn we cannot rightly handle the jus-

39. This freakishness runs through every criminal code. In Ohio, *e.g.*, torturing a child and cheating at cards are both offenses. Cheating where less than $150 is involved is a misdemeanor of the first degree, as is the simple torture of a child, without ensuing "serious physical harm." Cheating is a felony of the fourth degree when $150 or more is involved, as is torturing a child with resultant "serious physical harm." Ohio Rev. Code Ann. §§2915.05, 2919.22 (Baldwin 1975). Accidentally torturing a child to death would not be aggravated murder, or even murder. See text at note 8 *supra*. Do all these things represent serious moral judgments? Was sitting in the car while Cohen was accidentally killed worse than accidentally torturing a child to death, by going a little further than you intended?

40. See Roberts v. Louisiana, 96 S. Ct. 3001, 3007–08 (1976); Woodson v. North Carolina, 96 S. Ct. 2978, 2991–92 (1976).

41. Furman v. Georgia, 408 U.S. 238 (1972).

42. See note 2, p. 136 in this book.

tice of death, but stammer in dilemma before the mystery.

People sometimes ask me, "Would you be for capital punishment if you were sure it were being administered with perfect fairness?" The short answer, of course, is that I would not, as the questioner, desiring to embarrass me, well knows. But what I cannot see is why people think this should embarrass me. The radical incapacity of human justice to handle this business right is only a lesser included case of its intrinsic wrongness—or at the very most is in no way inconsistent with the latter view.

But something else is wrong, deeply wrong, with this question. One could ask, "Would you take trains if the earth were made flat, or would you fear they would run off the edge?" I cannot assert for absolute sure that technology, even in my life, may not be adequate to flattening out the earth, gently enough to leave me alive. But why would we be talking about that now?

Let us not bother too much, now, about what we would do if the earth were made flat, or if π were a rational number, or if we had a system of justice that could come within far calling distance of administering the death penalty with that divinely scrupulous and infallible fairness needed for resolving upon the killing of a person by law.

No. Let us think instead about a real world, a real legal system, real cases. For now, with me, think about Sandra Lockett.

Chapter 3

Reflections on Opposing the Penalty of Death (1978)*

FOR ABOUT five years now, I have been going up and down the land, in print sometimes but mostly not in print, trying to persuade my fellow citizens that the penalty of death ought to be abolished. For most of that time, I have mainly stressed a single thesis. In this talk I want, first, to try to place that thesis, a little more definitely than I have done before, in relation to other lines of thought about the death penalty, and then to say a very little about certain other reflections of mine on the theme, without quite as definite a relation to what has become, one might say, my principal specialty as a part of the opposition to this practice.

* Delivered January 19, 1978, at St. Mary's School of Law.

I mean this to be a self-contained talk, because it would be both vain and unrealistic to assume that everybody here has read my previous writings on this subject. I shall therefore state, as briefly as I can, what I have been trying to say in the main body of that work.

Whatever may have been the case in the past, the death penalty for a long time has been and definitely promises to continue being administered by a system that is characterized by a large amount of arbitrariness and mistake-proneness. Those who are to die have been chosen by a process which, at every critical stage, proceeds on no clearly articulated or understandable criteria. This starts with the stage of charging and pleading; the decision of the prosecutor as to what to charge and as to whether to offer a plea-bargain is not only unfettered and unreviewable but also without any clear and authoritative standards for the exercise of discretion. The luck of the draw in the jury is what I have called it, the luck of the draw. In a great majority of cases, the jury is instructed upon and may find "guilty" upon a lesser included offense, rather than on the charge that makes the defendant eligible for death; there is no review of this decision, and even instruction from the bench upon the difference between first- and second-degree murder, on premeditation, on the provocation that justifies or compels a manslaughter finding, and so on, is necessarily vague, for the law itself is vague. The "insanity defense," allowed in every state but in no state given a really intelligible definition, is a wild joker in the deck. At the separate sentencing stage, the state statutes, most of them recently put in place, contain other wild jokers which make unfaultable and unreviewable a decision for death or against death at this point. The decision for or against clemency is designedly standardless. The net effect is that virtually full discretion exists, taking the system as a whole, to select or not to select the particular defendant, out of the very many who might have been eligible, for suffering the supreme agony. Such a system, it seems to me, is not good enough for making this choice.

Now I am going to do what might seem a most arrogant thing, though I believe that on reflection you will not find it so. I am going to ask that tentatively, and for this short time only, we assume that the foregoing is a correct description of the system by which eligibility for death is established and acted upon. I make this quite temporary draft upon your patience and kindness because my aim in this talk is not to reargue this thesis but rather to place it in relation to other thoughts and questions about the penalty of death.

I must only add, by way of proëmium, that my remarks will be somewhat personal, because they originate, in greatest part, as reactions to various questions I have met throughout the country, and as quite personal thoughts of my own—mostly, I must confess, while jogging my daily five miles, an ordeal that may prolong life as far as cardiac problems are concerned, but that soon would kill with boredom if one did not think furiously and continuously over a wide range of subjects.

Now the first thing I have noticed, as I have gone about preaching the thesis I have just stated, is that many persons in my audiences seem to have been making an order-of-magnitude mistake as to what it was that was being asserted. Often, a questioner seems under the impression that what I have said is that there are certain small though definite defects in our choice-for-death system, certain problems around its edges, whereas what I have been saying is that it is riddled up and down, through and through, with major vaguenesses and indeterminacies, and with major possibilities of error, where there is a standard clear enough for the concept of "error" to be meaningful. This is a matter of mere misunderstanding, perhaps connected with an inability to believe that things can really be all that awry as to so terrible a matter, regardless of what we know of human fallibility and of original sin.

More serious is a questioning along lines which may be exemplified by the query, "But what would be your position if the system of choosing persons for death were perfect?" I have reflected much on the implications of this question, and I will now explore some of these: this will in fact be the main organizing principle of my talk here.

First of all, for candor ought to come first, is my literal answer: "I would be against the penalty of death no matter how perfected the system for administering it might be." I have given this answer on many occasions. Let me first admit how personal such an opinion is, and then add how personal must be all opinions of this sort, upon which, in their sum, our moral life rests. I will make my point by telling you a true story.

Last November, in Washington, I found myself in the company of fourteen philosophers. I am not myself philosophically learned, and as they had at me I sometimes felt that their number—fourteen—was not accidental, but constituted a jury, with the two alternates now customary; once, when I had to leave the room, I returned in some fear of the verdict. Seriously, however, they pressed me very hard for a cogent demonstration, a proof in moral philosophy, of the wrongness of the punishment of death. Of course I had none; it will not do, for example, to refer to the harrowing pages of Camus and Koestler, where the degrading horror of the practice is made real to the mind, for the philosophers could, and did, simply say, "But how do you prove *that* wrong?" But I finally had a very simple inspiration. I said to them, "Pick anything you choose, of which *you* disapprove—the boiling in oil of some murderers in Tudor or Stuart England, the penalty of hanging, drawing and quartering, the *amende honorable* inflicted on the attempter upon Louis XV's life, the burnings at the stake performed by both sides in the religious wartime of the sixteenth century, crucifixion as practiced by the Romans. There must be something in all this that you are prepared to call wrong. Now pick that thing, and construct for me a proof in moral philosophy that it *is* wrong. Then I will know what such a demonstration looks like, and I will see whether I can construct one to show that the infliction of death by judgment of law is wrong."

Of course the subject was forthwith changed; no such demonstration was any more possible in their mouths than in mine, and yet not one of them would have hesitated to condemn most or all of the practices I referred to.

I think that, if philosophy were a more rigorous discipline, it would long ago have been proved, to everybody's satisfaction, that no such demonstration is possible, in the end, of a moral judgment. Those who, like me, oppose the penalty of death altogether, are simply making the judgment that it is too much, too cruel, too degrading to the offender and to society. We cannot prove this, but neither can the opponent of bone-breaking as a prelude to crucifixion prove his case. The two opinions stand upon exactly the same logical or scientific footing. Our part of the world, the western Christian part,[1] has by and large decided that torture is

---

1. This expression was inadvertent. Japan amongst other countries not answering this description has abolished the penalty of death, and of course does not practice torture.

just too much, no matter what the offense. Four hundred years ago that decision had not been made. No new rational arguments have been devised in the meanwhile, coercing the mind to the judgment that torture is too much, whatever the offense may have been. The change from the sixteenth century's opinion on torture to the twentieth century's opinion on torture is not at all like the change from the sixteenth century's belief as to the age of the earth to the twentieth century's belief on the same subject. The torture change is a shift of the moral emotions, of conscience—not of the intellect.

Now if we look over the history of the whole world during the last century, we perceive in progress, I think, a similar world-wide shift with regard to the death penalty. Like all historical currents, this one may change. Those of us who are opposing the death penalty in America are engaged in attempting to persuade others that we should join rather than oppose this shift in moral feeling. But on the principal and final issue itself—the inherent and intrinsic wrongness of the death penalty—neither we nor our adversaries can, strictly speaking, adduce rational arguments. The most we can do is to expose the penalty to view, in all its compound horror as we perceive it, and invite others, informed by this view, to agree. Koestler and Camus, chiefly among many others, have done this, performing (as one reviewer of my own book put it) the "emotional act" of exhibiting the penalty as it is and as it is felt by those who suffer it.

In my own case, I have elected not to do this over again. It has seemed to me that I, as a lawyer, could make a different contribution—the exhibiting to view of the multiple arbitrarinesses of the process by which people have been and are being chosen to suffer this agony. And the charge I seem to be encountering here and

there—and I use the word "seem" because it is a charge
never clearly spelled out—is that there is some kind of inconsistency in my being, at once, a convinced opponent
of the death penalty however administered, and also an
advocate of the view that the processes by which we
select those who die are riddled with arbitrariness and
mistake-proneness.

I can see one grain of truth in this charge—or,
rather, one sense in which it might be true. It might be
said that one who is resolutely opposed to the death penalty, however administered, is not the best judge of the
adequacy of the procedure by which it is administered.
That is perhaps right, but not responsive to the actual
state of the argument. I am not merely registering my
own judgment on the nature of the death-penalty system.
I have been describing that system by drawing attention
to its publicly knowable characteristics, inviting the
judgment of readers and hearers—without, of course,
concealing my own judgment. Every assertion I make is
subject to easy disaffirmance if it be false. So far as I am
aware, no serious attempt has been made to perform this
disaffirmance. But even if everything I have asserted is
true, nobody else's judgment can be coerced to the final
act of rejection. In the end of ends, final judgment here
cannot be rational, though it can be informed by
reason—or, more humbly, by knowledge of the facts—at
all stages short of finality. One must at last judge whether
such a system as we have will decently do for selecting
whom to kill by law.

Beyond this point, I cannot see how my own opposition to the death penalty as a thing in itself can taint or
touch my contention that, even if you believe in the penalty as a thing in itself, you ought to consider whether the
process by which it is administered is not so flawed as to

make morally necessary its abandonment. I think of a conversation. Someone says, "I am opposed to the penalty of death. It is too horrible a thing for all of us to do to any of us." Someone answers,, "Well, I don't agree." The first speaker then says, "I won't try to argue you out of that view, for it is in the end unarguable, but won't you consider whether even someone, who—like you—does not disapprove of the death penalty in the abstract, can approve of the system by which people are actually chosen to die? Let me tell you a little about that system." I confess I absolutely fail to understand how the person who says this—and this is what I have been saying—is even close to inconsistency.

But let me now enter another area into which I am led by this question. I will open this branch of my remarks by going back to my fourteen philosophers. They were most interested—and, as philosophers, they must be—in the abstract question of the rightness of the death penalty. The discussion, for a time, proceeded on this level. At this level, such terms as "those who deserve to die," or "the relation of man to the state," were freely used. At one point, I made the only intervention a lawyer could make, by saying, "Ladies and gentlemen, it is no doubt well that philosophers never cease from pondering the great abstract questions of the universe, from the nature of being on down. But if you want to discuss the *political* question facing the United States today, you cannot use such a term as 'those who deserve to die' without an interlinear gloss, or a footnote, *every time* you use the term, explaining that by 'those who deserve to die' you mean 'those who are found to deserve to die by the criminal justice system as it stands and as it operates.' This is a ponderous gloss, and may tend to interrupt the flow of discourse and dull its elegance, but these disadvantages are as nothing when compared with the disadvantage of failing to keep steadily present in mind the fact that all we are now discussing and can discuss is the question whether those persons shall be killed who are chosen for death by our system as it stands."

I will say that, from this encounter and others, it seems to me that one of the chief troubles, if not the chief trouble, with most philosophizing about law is that it fails to be utterly permeated, as all useful thought about law must be permeated, by consciousness and concrete knowledge of *process*. I venture to hope, though not quite to predict, that a whole new school of the philosophy of law may one day arise, based centrally upon the operational or processual approach. After all, it is entirely possible to state verbally a hypothetical case in which two events in far-separated galaxies occur simultaneously. Modern physics tells us, I think, that such a case would contain a meaningless term—"simultaneity"—because no operations or observations can be planned or executed which would make it possible to use this term in a meaningful way. I would be glad to see a philosophy of legal "fact" which was based upon there being, strictly speaking, no such thing as "fact," but only testimony, and procedures for settling upon a verbal account which will be *regarded* as stating, authoritatively, the "facts" of a case. I would like to see what could be done with a philosophy of the law of contracts which started from the rather obvious truth that, where experienced and learned persons can disagree on the meaning of words, those words have no single meaning, but only the demonstrated potentiality of carrying two or more meanings—a potentiality that may be acted upon, but cannot be altered by, the processes of legal "interpretation." "Law" is not norms-plus-process but process wherein norms play such part as they can in the process given. But let me bring this thought back to my main theme here.

On that theme, then: The question I have just put—the question whether it is right to kill such people as are chosen by our system as it stands—is not a peripheral or side-question. It is not a needless complication of a simple question, or a needlessly confusing combination of two separate questions. It is the *only* question that actually confronts us. We are not presently confronted, as a political society, with the question whether something called "the state" has some abstract right to kill "those who deserve to die." We are confronted by the single unitary question posed by reality: "Shall we kill those who are chosen to be killed by our legal process as it stands?" My own work has been principally devoted to trying to throw more light on one aspect of that single unitary question—that part of it which invites inquiry as to the nature of the system as it stands. Strictly, for this purpose, it doesn't really make any difference at all what I think about the abstract rightness of capital punishment. There exists no abstract capital punishment.

Of course, it might be said that the single unitary question that now confronts us might change its aspect very quickly, by drastic improvements in the systems for choosing those who are to die. But the present systems, out in the states, are the best the states have been able to come up with in the years since the Furman case, against a far longer background of thought and experience. Their defects, in process and in concepts that work themselves out only in process, are deeply rooted in the law of decades and even of centuries past. There is not, realistically, the smallest chance of major improvement, *transforming* improvement, in any time soon to come. And even if there were, we are confronted right now with the question of sending to death row or not sending to death row, killing or not killing, persons already chosen or in the process of being chosen by the systems as they stand. Not even the most optimistic looker-forward can avoid or evade this question.

Yet I am now myself in what I might loosely call a philosophic vein, and I cannot restrain myself from talking to you about the deepest of the thoughts that have come to me from being asked, perhaps five hundred times, "Would you favor the death penalty if it were administered by a perfect system?" My own philosophic depths, which are, I am afraid, rather shallow as philosophic depths go, have finally been stirred to produce the counter-question, "What can this person mean by a 'perfect system'?" And here, again, the dominant theme must be the *processual* theme. It is impossible to stress this too strongly, or too often.

I can sketch imaginatively, though in the pale tones of utter political impossibility, some aspects of the system which could be brought to something that might be called perfection, as human perfection goes. For example—and I know what a ludicrous example it is, in the world we actually live in—it is imaginable that every capital defendant might be furnished by the state, at every stage, with the best counsel money can buy, and with completely adequate funds for investigation, for expert witnesses, and for everything else that you or I would hock our souls to get if we had anyone dear to us standing accused of a capital offense. Since we would all do this, presumably we consider it advantageous to have and to use these resources. By clearest consequence, we must consider it disadvantageous not to have them. When I got off the plane recently in a Western state, some people were falling all over me to let me know that there were three men currently in the death house there without any lawyers at all to prepare their federal appeal papers—and time was running. Thinking of that situation, and many others like it, I almost laugh at what I am about to say. But I can at least imagine that a civilized state might decide that, before leading a person into a small room to be killed, it should afford the best, and not the grudgingly conceded bedrock minimum, of resources for making a defense. If that were to be done, the system would be, in that one aspect alone, perfected.

Even as to this kind of perfectibility, I wonder why anybody wants to raise the question now. I have always been patient on these occasions, but I find it difficult to treat this question as anything but diversionary. You raise the terrible question, "Shall we kill poor people who have been furnished minimal legal representation and next to no other resources for preparing a defense?" and the reply is, "What would you say if the state furnished each capital defendant with means actually sufficient for putting up the best possible defense?" Is it possible that the questioner is not seeking, consciously or unconsciously, to direct the attention—his own attention, perhaps—away from one aspect of the terrible, and terribly real, issue that actually confronts him, and me, and all of us?

On many other questions of perfectibility, or even of susceptibility of improvement, I am not so sure I may even imagine what the questioner means, or supply a meaning for him. Here, again, attention to processual issues brings some clarity.

Let us take the simplest plane—that of fact. What does it mean to speak of a "perfect" system in this regard? That predication has no operational meaning unless a better, more reliable system is used to check factual determinations, but what is the guarantee that this system

itself possesses infallibility, or any given degree of rightness? (Of course such a system is merely imaginary.)

But this is rather abstract. Let's take a middling-
complicated question of mixed physical and psychological fact, coupled with a normative judgment: "Did the
defendant kill the victim because of a reasonable belief
that his own life was threatened?" Now no improvement
in the legal system is ever going to enable the fact-finding
tribunal to witness personally even the external events
under examination. Whether the deceased pulled a
knife, or looked as if he were going to pull a knife, is all a
matter of inference from testimony, very often the testimony of the defendant, and in other cases almost always
the testimony, given much later, of witnesses to a rapidly
moving, exciting course of events. Whether the defendant believed the victim had a knife is a question of
psychological fact, but of great difficulty of investigation.
Whether the belief was "reasonable" is a matter of ad hoc
evaluation by a jury. How can all this be changed?

A level deeper, we come to the pure question of
mental state and its evaluation. I put the matter in that
general way because I am aware that some now favor the
doing away with the so-called insanity defense. But I
cannot imagine that any moral society could look on
mental state as totally irrelevant to the question whether
death was deserved as a penalty. Yet I cannot imagine,
either, how the techniques for dealing with this, with
which our legal culture has without success struggled for
so long, could be refined so as to eliminate arbitrariness
and mistake from judgment.

In Brooklyn recently, a white policeman shot and
killed, apparently without provocation, a black youth of
fifteen. The defense, supported by medical testimony,
was that the policeman had suffered a sudden psycholog-

ical seizure or episode. The jury acquitted. I do not
impugn their judgment; it may well have been right. But
what I ask you to consider is what the chances would be
of a black youth who, without provocation, shot and
killed a policeman, and proferred the same defense.
Wherever the verbal line is drawn, and under whatever
name, between those states of mind which qualify for
death and those which do not, arbitrariness and mistake
will continue to rule.

Sometimes I think the question, "What would you
do if the death-choice system were perfected?" is like the
question, "What would you do if 40 percent of the people
in the United States learned to speak pretty good Japanese
by next New Year's Day?"—a question that states an
hypothesis not physically impossible, not even psycholog-
ically impossible case by case, but absolutely impossible
from the social and political point of view. But sometimes I think the question is more like, "What would you
do if an amoeba were taught to play the piano?" I daresay
the question concerns a mixture of both these things—
the politically and socially impossible, and the rigorously
impossible even to the imagination.

Let me turn to the very closely connected
question—the question of the actual existence of mistake
in death cases. It must be conceded that there are very
few instances of established mistake in cases where execution has occurred. But I think that on reflection you
may agree with me that this is, literally, quite meaningless—and I choose that word carefully. Such reflection
must, again, attend to *processual* issues.

First, and perhaps most important, there are in our
legal system no procedures or tribunals or jurisdictions
for "establishing" that someone should not, under law,
have suffered death. When one says that there are few

"established" cases of this wrong, what is he talking about? Many people think a mistake was made in the famous Rosenberg case. But where do they file the papers, for an official declaration? The mere publication of new evidence, or of new views about the evidence, "establishes" nothing. This is to be strongly contrasted with the situation as to imprisonment, where there is always a real party in interest to move for a new trial; there are exceedingly weighty difficulties about such a motion, but it is at least a possibility.

Secondly, there is a lack of the energizing effect of there being something tangible that can be accomplished by demonstrating mistake. A person in prison wants out. His family and friends want him out. How many resources can be devoted to mere name-clearing by the relatives and friends of those men whom I just mentioned, who could hardly get lawyers to prepare their federal papers while they were still alive?

But the difficulty is vastly deeper. For our society is totally committed to executing, not *all* who have committed homicide, but only *some*, selected in accordance with certain procedures and certain criteria. If these procedures err, if these criteria are incorrectly applied, then "mistake" *as to execution* has occurred. And the trouble is that, through virtually their entire range, these subsidiary criteria, the ones actually set up for the death choice, are either exceedingly difficult of establishment, so that a jury's verdict, even if based on a guess, can hardly be definitely faulted, or are too lacking in meaning for the concept of "mistake" to apply.

Let me go back to the defense of "reasonable belief that one's life is endangered." Only a belief in direct divine guidance of the jury could lead anyone to think that the verdict on this is always right. But try to imagine how one would, after execution, go about faulting that verdict.

Or, to revert to a deeper level, all states, including Texas, are committed to not executing persons as to whom there exists some mitigating mental or psychic condition, usually referred to as the "insanity defense." Let's go back to the case of the policeman who shot the fifteen-year-old boy. His insanity defense was submitted to the jury, and they bought it. But if they hadn't, and if he had been executed—as would be possible in some states—how would one go about *establishing* that this was a mistake? Of course there is no way; this is so clear that your first reaction might be to think the question silly. If that is what you think, I think it is because the "insanity defense" typically poses a question which is not in fact understood by either the judge or the jury. Of course one cannot at a later time establish "mistake" as to the answer to this question, when that answer has resulted in the killing by law of the defendant. Neither can one establish the correctness of the answer.

Some states are committed to refraining from executing people convicted under the felony-murder doctrine, where the defendant's participation in the felony was "relatively minor." Some states are committed to considering the defendant's "age" or "youth." These questions are typical of the question so vague that no answer can be established as wrong, or right. Of course "mistake" cannot be established as to the answers to such questions, and could not be established even if a tribunal existed charged with that responsibility. But what does that tell us as to the nature of the question?

Or take, for a final example, your famous Texas "Question 2," asked of the jury at the punishment hearing. The jury must determine "beyond a reasonable doubt" that "there is a probability that the defendant would commit criminal acts of violence that would constitute a continuing threat to society. . . ."

I have examined this question from many sides in previous writings. What I am saying now is that, if there is any seriousness in law or life, Texas has quite seriously committed herself *not* to kill persons as to whom this question ought to be answered "no." An execution in such a case is a mistaken execution. But try to imagine how one would go about establishing, after the execution, that a mistake had been made—or had not been made.

I think the upshot of all this is that, in greatest part, the concept of "establishment of mistaken execution" simply evaporates. No tribunals, no procedures, no tangible energizing motivation, and no sufficient concepts exist for performing this act of "establishment." This again is a point at which abstraction from process is fatal to understanding, or to meaningful conclusions.

I have spoken at length, and only touched a few points of interest to me—and I hope to you. The room is endless for reflection on this penalty. Those who, like me, oppose it can ask no more than that you reflect upon it; this reflection on your part is in the end our only chance of victory.

I will say only one more thing. One tries, after many years of living, to look back and make some sense of one's life, or of major parts of one's life. As I have looked back on my work in law, I have asked myself: "What does it all add up to? What unity is there in it?"

I haven't the answer to all of it yet, and doubtless never will. But I do see the connection, I think, between my work in combatting racism and my work in fighting against the penalty of death. And this connection is at a level far deeper than would be suggested by the mere fact that a largely disproportionate number of black people are and have been on death row, as disturbing and shameful as that fact is.

I have carried around in my heart, since I read it, Albert Camus's saying that the infliction of capital punishment violates the only genuine human community—the community in the face of death. And I have never forgotten James Baldwin's being sorrowfully amazed that it could be, in the face of the death that waits for all of us, the last going down of the sun, that some people could treat other people so shamefully, because of the colors of their skins. To me, the truth behind these sayings is one. The penalty of death, and the cruel injustice of racism, violate our bedrock community—the community of all people, all of whom must face death together. And I suppose that is the deepest root of my own motives in these central parts of my own work in law. Or very near to the deepest.